L

Make ... **time!**

JOHANN
SEBASTIAN
BACH

VISIT THE CITY

BKB Verlag

LEIPZIG AT A GLANCE

A City Stroll

Mus. d Bild. Künste

Plagwitz

Battle of the Nations Monument

Strolling and Shopping

3 Days in

Content

Legend

- ⧖ Duration of the tour
- ◆ Opening times/ departure times
- ▲ Transport stop
- ➤ see

Editor:
Dr. Brigitte Hintzen-Bohlen

Layout:
Andreas Ossig
BKB Verlag GmbH

Translation:
John Sykes

Printing:
Brandt GmbH, Bonn

ISBN 978-3-940914-69-9

All contents and information have been conscientiously researched and carefully checked. Nevertheless it is not always possible to avoid errors entirely. We are therefore pleased to receive corrections and proposals for additions.

BKB Verlag GmbH
Auerstrasse 4
50733 Köln
Telephone   +49 (0)221/9521460
Telefax   +49 (0)221/5626446
www.bkb-verlag.de
mail@bkb-verlag.de

Welcome to

... an old city of commerce and trade fairs, symbolised by a double M that remains the emblem of the city to this day. It stands for a marketplace that was established as early as the 12th century, grew rapidly following the imperial trade fair privilege of 1467 and continues today thanks to the modern trade fair centre. It is synonymous with tradition and renewal, which have always been closely linked in Leipzig. This is the place where Bach and Mendelssohn composed music, Goethe created the figure of Faust, and Leibniz, Nietzsche and Kästner studied. Countless publishing houses were based here before the war, and the peaceful revolution of 1989 started with the Monday demonstrations in Leipzig.

Leipzig ...

Leipzig is at one and the same time a city of trade fairs and a university, of music and books, but it was always the citizens who made Leipzig what it is. They supported fine arts and sciences from an early stage in the city history, which is why Leipzig can boast one of the most beautiful of all Renaissance city halls and, with the Gewandhaus Orchestra, one of the world's most famous ensembles. Donations made it possible to build the art gallery and opera house, and the trading houses of rich merchants have today been transformed into magnificent arcades. Little Paris, in fact, to use Goethe's just words of praise.

Today Leipzig is a lively and vibrant city, bursting with confidence, and has grown enormously, mainly thanks to an increase in young residents. The appearance of the city is still marked by exciting contrasts: magnificent burghers' houses, some beautifully restored and others in decay, wasteland next to palaces of glass, prefabricated high-rises next to Classical architecture, Art Nouveau and Post-Modern styles side by side. Above all Leipzig is characterised by its cultural life, with the choir of St Thomas' Church, the Gewandhaus Orchestra, cabarets, avant-garde theatre and the new arts scene in the west of the city. And don't forget the Saxon love of life: there are inviting street cafés and "free seats", as beer gardens are known here, everywhere you look, and the locals have a friendly, optimistic way of life. Welcome!

About Leipzig

● Leipzig is home to the world's oldest and most extensive RAIL TERMINUS: in 2001 the Bayerischer Bahnhof, the oldest surviving rail terminus in the world, was closed. Since then Leipziger Gose, a kind of beer with a slightly sour taste, has been brewed and drunk here. The new main station, with an area of 83,640 square metres and 23 platforms, is Europe's largest rail terminus.

● At 114 metres, the city-hall tower of the NEUES RATHAUS is Germany's tallest.

● Only the south entrance to the new City-Tunnel-Station Leipzig serves as a reminder of the UNDERGROUND TRADE-FAIR HOUSE that was built beneath the market in 1924 as there was a shortage of exhibition space. It was the world's only subterranean trade-fair building.

● From the monument to the Battle of the Nations you can look down on the chapel of Germany's second-largest park cemetery, the SÜD-FRIEDHOF, which is over 130 years old and has mature trees on an area of some 80 hectares. Many important persons from Leipzig – business people, scientists, artists and architects – have been laid to rest here.

● Europe's longest building inscription, at 96 words, can be seen around the ALTES RATHAUS, built in 1556–57. It expresses the thanks of the city to the sponsors and to God.

● Leipzig is a green city. 950 hectares of ancient FLOODPLAIN FOREST extend through its urban surroundings.

● In the countryside around Leipzig, once marked by mining, the Leipzig NEUSEENLAND has been created. This newly made landscape of 22 lakes has a total water surface amounting to almost 70 square kilometres.

● The first PHYSICS INSTITUTE at a German university was founded by Gustav Theodor Fechner (1801-87) at Leipzig University.

● When Vladimir Putin was based in Leipzig from 1985 to 1990 as a KGB agent, the pub where he was a regular was the old-established GOSENSCHENKE called Ohne Bedenken. "Cajari's Darling", a pork steak with hot liver sausage and fried potatoes, is said to have been his favourite dish.

● Since 1972 Leipzig Zoo has kept the INTERNATIONAL TIGER BREEDING BOOK, in which the details of all the tigers in zoos, circuses and safari parks across the whole world are recorded.

● In the BELANTIS fun park, the largest in all of eastern Germany, the Huracan rollercoaster with a free fall from a height of 32 metres and five loops is among the top ten of the world's steepest rollercoaster rides.

● In 1897 the first MARATHON RUN in Germany was held in Leipzig when the club Sportsbrüder Leipzig organised a 40-km long-distance race from Paunsdorf to Bennewitz and back.

● The first of the TV crime stories in the TATORT series was set in Leipzig, produced by the north German broadcaster NDR, and shown in 1970 under the title Taxi to Leipzig.

● Leipzig was celebrated in 1989 as a HEROIC CITY because the Monday demonstrations provided a decisive impulse for the change of regime in the GDR.

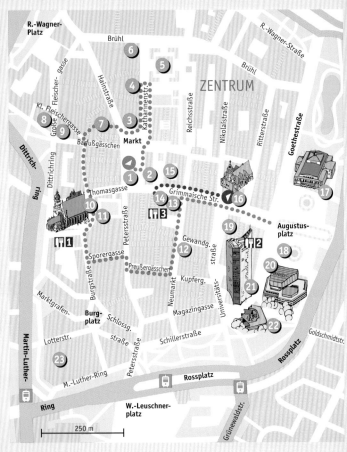

1. Königshaus
2. Old City Hall/City History Museum
3. Alte Waage
4. Fregehaus
5. Museum of Visual Arts
6. Romanushaus
7. Barthels Hof
8. Coffe Baum
9. Drallewatsch
10. St. Thomas Church
11. Bach-Museum
12. Städtisches Kaufhaus
13. Zeitgeschichtliches Forum
14. Mädlerpassage
15. Naschmarkt/Alte Börse
16. St. Nikolas' Church
17. Opera House
18. Mendebrunnen
19. University
20. Gewandhaus
21. City Hochhaus
22. Moritzbastei
23. New City Hall

1. Café Kandler
2. Panorama Tower
3. Auerbachs Keller

Day 1

A walk through the city centre

A City Stroll

Mus. d. Bild. Künste

3 Days in

Battle of the Nations Monument

Plagwitz

Strolling and Shopping

A WALK THROUGH THE CITY CENTRE – MERCHANTS, MUSICIANS AND DEMONSTRATORS

Hieronymus Lotter (1497–1580)

Moritzbastei, Pleissenburg, Altes Rathaus, Alte Waage – these are just a few of the buildings that are closely linked to the name of Hieronymus Lotter, the son of a cloth trader from Nuremberg. In 1522 Lotter, a successful merchant, came to Leipzig and rose to prominence as architect to the prince elector, and as alderman and mayor.

His career was meteoric, his fall precipitous: because of the delays in building Augustusburg Palace and the explosion in costs, Elector Augustus dismissed his architect without paying the amounts that Lotter had advanced. Lotter had to sell all his possessions and died a poor and lonely man.

On a walk through the city centre you can learn the difference between fairs for goods and fairs for samples, discover typical merchants' houses, see where the famous church musician Bach worked and find out about post-1945 history.

Marktplatz and Altes Rathaus

Markt 1, ◆ Tue–Sun 10am–6pm, Tour 1st Wed in month 5pm
www.stadtgeschichtliches-museum-leipzig.de

The starting point for this walk through the city centre is the marketplace (Marktplatz), where the city coat of arms is set into the mosaic paving. It is a popular rendezvous even when no market or event such as the city festival, the Classic Open or the famous Christmas market is taking place.

The marketplace is bordered by historic buildings that were rebuilt after wartime destruction and newer buildings reminiscent of the outline of the old ones. Note here the *Alte Waage* on the north side, in which all goods sold at the Leipzig fair had to be weighed and assessed for customs, and on the south side the *Königshaus*, rebuilt in Baroque style. The dominant building, on the east side, is the *Altes Rathaus* (old city hall), one of the most beautiful examples of German Renaissance architecture.

This long building with 24 window bays and six gables was erected in just nine months in 1556-57 by Hieronymus Lotter, the prince elector's architect and mayor of Leipzig. To lend this elongated structure an appearance of height, the clock tower, which was later made taller in the Baroque style, was not placed in the middle of the façade. From its balcony the city horn blowers once played the cornet and trumpet each day.

Since 1906 the *Stadtgeschichtliches Museum* (city history museum) has occupied the first floor. This fascinating journey through the ups and downs of the city shows the first municipal charter of 1156, the trade fair privilege of Emperor Maximilian and the contract that Bach signed as cantor of St Thomas' Church on 5 May 1723. The museum tells you everything from the beginnings of Leipzig to the Battle of the Nations, from the fair to the revolution of 1989.

Katharinenstrasse

To get an idea of Leipzig's glory as a trading city in its golden age, take a stroll through Katharinenstrasse. The tall merchants' houses on its west side survived the war undamaged. Their inner courtyards are connected to the neighbouring Hainstrasse via passageways (the modern Bildermuseum is opposite, ➤ p. 36). The Baroque *Fregehaus* (no. 11) with its lavishly decorated oriel in the central axis is conspicuous for its many dormers, which show the number of attic storeys.

The Baroque *Romanushaus* is especially impressive. It has two show fronts at the corner facing Bühl. Representations of Athena and Fama are seated above the entrance. It was built for Dr. Romanus, mayor of Leipzig, who introduced public street lighting and initiated public transport by employing sedan chair bearers, but was then kept under arrest for 41 years due to corruption in office.

Yards and passages

As a trading city needs lots of space for deliveries, storage and sales, Leipzig merchants' houses were built with "through-yards" for access: usually a house at the front and one or more buildings in the yards behind were strung out along the plot and connected by a narrow

passage, which made it possible to load goods quickly without turning the cart. The fair transactions took place in the ground-floor vaults. Counting houses and living quarters occupied the floors above, and goods were stored in the tall attics. In the Baroque period the uniformly designed "through-houses" developed from this. Both types of building survive today as covered arcades.

Drallewatsch ...

... is a Saxon dialect word meaning *to go out* or *step it out*, and the people of Leipzig use it to describe their entertainment quarter around Barfussgasse, Fleischergasse and Klostergasse. Places to dance, eat and drink, from established restaurants to trendy bars, are thick on the ground here. In winter a colourful mix of guests throng inside, and in summer each crowded alley becomes a "freisitz" (a Saxon word for a beer garden or terrace). For all the fun down below, don't forget to look up at the historic buildings from the Renaissance, Baroque period and the 19th century.

Barthels Hof
Hainstrasse 1
www.barthels-hof.de

An example of a splendid merchant's house is the courtyard house built by Gottlieb Barthel in the 18th century. Here four-storey buildings are arranged round a through-yard. On the roof storeys look out for the crane beams with which goods were hoisted up to the storage space. The Renaissance oriel with a gold snake is an unusual feature. It was moved to the inner courtyard from the previous building of 1523, called the *Golden Snake*.

Coffe Baum
Kleine Fleischergasse 4
◆ *Museum 11am–7pm, free admission, tour 1. Tue in the month 5 pm*

On the little square in Drallewatsch a white, five-storey Renaissance house catches the eye. It is home to one of the oldest coffee houses in Europe. Coffee, chocolate and tea have been served here since 1711. The name, *Zum Arabischen Coffe Baum*, is a description of the Baroque relief above the entrance, on which a sumptuously dressed oriental wearing a turban offers coffee to a putto beneath a flowering coffee tree.

Those interesting in learning more about Saxon coffee-drinking culture will find historical and curious items in the museum, from Meissen porcelain for coffee to the coffee cup from which Napoleon drank in 1813.

Bach-Museum
Thomaskirchhof 15/16
◆ *Tue-Sun 10am-6pm, www.bachmuseumleipzig.de*

Walk along Klostergasse to reach a place closely associated with Johann Sebastian Bach, one of the most famous citizens of Leipzig. An exhibition in the historical Bose house is devoted specially to the life and work of this great composer

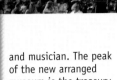

and musician. The peak of the new arranged museum is the treasury with autograph Bach-handwritings.

Thomaskirche
Thomaskirchhof 18
◆ *9am–6pm*
www.thomaskirche.org

Nowhere is Bach than closer in the Thomaskirche (St Thomas' Church), which was his home from home in Leipzig. Whatever is being performed, *Jesu, Joy of Man's Desiring* or the *St Matthew Passion*, a motet or a chorale, there is no more impressive place to enjoy a concert of his works: every Friday at 6 pm and Saturday at 3 pm you have the opportunity. The Thomaskirche, which was rebuilt as a late Gothic hall church up to 1496 and later gained a Baroque tower, has a tradition of music going back over 800 years. The famous boys' choir of St Thomas (Thomanerchor) was founded with the first church in the 12th century, and Bach conducted it when he was cantor of St Thomas. There are reminders of the great composer on every side: a statue of him stands in the churchyard, a portrait adorns one of the windows on the south side of the church, and his mortal remains rest below a bronze tomb-cover in the chancel. Apart from that the church interior is austere, as all works of art were removed in 1539 during the Reformation. This is why the beautiful 15th-century winged altar from St Paul's Church (➤ p. 16), which shows the apostle Paul surrounded by scenes from the New Testament, has only been here for a few years.

> **»Have a break«** 🚶1
> Bachtaler, coffee and cake are good reasons to take a break at **Café Kandler**.
> *Thomaskirchhof 11*
> ◆ *10am–8pm*

The 17th cantor of St Thomas
When the position of cantor of St Thomas and musical director of Leipzig was vacant in 1723, Johann Sebastian Bach was not the first choice. Perhaps this was the reason why he brought a blaze of energy to

his tasks of performing a cantata every Sunday and on every holiday, teaching at St Thomas' School and from 1729 conducting the Collegium Musicum of students. Or maybe his permanent conflicts with the city council about financial support for church music were the reason. By the time of his death in 1750, he had written some 300 cantatas and such famous works as his *St Matthew Passion*, *Christmas Oratorio* and *The Art of Fugue*, which have a permanent place in music history.

13

The mother of all trade fairs

The bronze statue of Emperor Maximilian I on Universitätsstrasse is a reminder of the imperial fair privilege of 1497, according to which no other town within a radius of about 115 kilometres was permitted to hold a fair. After this Leipzig, favourably located at the junction of two trade routes, became a leading place for commerce and fairs. For almost 400 years the Leipzig Fair was purely a goods fair, at which the goods on show were bought and sold on the spot. The change to a sample fair, where industrial goods were presented by dealers in the form of samples and delivered later, did not take place until 1895 (➤ p. 39).

Städtisches Kaufhaus (municipal trading house)
Neumarkt 9-19

Via Burgstrasse and narrow lanes continue to the building that reflects the commercial and cultural history of Leipzig as no other. It occupies the site of the late Gothic trade fair building that was known as the *Gewandhaus* (cloth house) because the first floor was used by the cloth and wool dealers. It was once the home of the orchestra of the same name. 250 years later part of it was demolished to build a Baroque municipal library, which itself was used for the trade fair from the late 19th century. This was the time when the change from a goods fair to a sample fair was taking place, and thus in 1894 construction of a new building, the world's first to be designed for a sample fair, began.

Its layout around a large inner courtyard and two light wells, which forced visitors to make a circuit of all the exhibitions on all floors, made it the model for later fair buildings in Leipzig. Today this neo-Baroque edifice is a modern office and retail property, and only the lift of 1901 in stairway A serves as a reminder of bygone days.

Zeitgeschichtliches Forum
Grimmaische Strasse 6
◆ *Tue–Fri 9am–6pm, Sat–Sun 10am–6pm, free admission*
www.hdg.de

This museum in the former central building of the trade fair is an invitation to take a critical look at German contemporary history from the end of the Second World War to the present. On an area of 2000 square metres it presents a journey in time to the history of the dictatorship and resistance in the Soviet-occupied zone and the GDR, commemorating opposition, resistance and civic courage.

The partition of Germany after the end of the Second World War, the uprising of 17 June 1953 and the building of the Berlin Wall in 1961, the invasion of Czechoslovakia in 1968, the expulsion of the singer-songwriter Wolf Biermann in 1976, the Monday demonstrations and the fall of the Wall in 1989, the successes and difficulties of the process of German reunification – no topic is left out. Leipzig, as the city whose residents shook the foundations of the authoritarian regime of the GDR with their peaceful revolution, seems the inevitable choice as the site of an outstation of the *House of History* in Bonn.

Naschmarkt ("munch market")

Diagonally opposite, at the back of the Altes Rathaus (old city hall), is a small square on which fruit and vegetables were sold in the Middle Ages. Today a medieval-style market is held only at Christmas and Easter as a reminder of its history as a place for trading. At its centre stands a statue of the young *Johann Wolfgang Goethe*, a student in Leipzig from 1765 to 1768. The two faces adorning the lower reliefs are those of Friedrike Oeser and Käthchen Schönkopf, two young ladies well known to Goethe.

Behind it a magnificent Baroque building with a double stairway catches the eye. Above its entrance two putti hold the coat of arms of the city of Leipzig. This is the *Alte Handelsbörse*, the old exchange, the place where merchants came together to conclude business and to hold assemblies and festivities. Today the former exchange hall is used for cultural events and receptions.

9 October 1989
Although the police blocked access roads to the Nikolaikirche (St Nicholas' Church) from May 1989 to make it more difficult to take part in the Monday prayers for peace, more and more people came. The flashpoint was on

7 October 1989, the 40th anniversary of the GDR, when countless defenceless persons were beaten and arrested. The state made a show of strength: the next Monday about 600 Party members occupied the church as early as 2 pm. However, the people of Leipzig were not to be cowed: pastor Christian Führer eventually even read out an appeal against violence by Kurt Masur, conductor of the Gewandhaus Orchestra, and tens of thousands of people waited outside holding lighted candles. The peaceful revolution was now irresistible, and the Wall fell just a month later, on 9 November.

Nikolaikirche

Nikolaikirchhof 3 ♦ 10am–6pm,
www.nikolaikirche.de

This Gothic hall church with a striking octagonal central tower by Hieronymus Lotter (1555), is known above all as the place where the peaceful revolution of 1989 in the GDR originated. This historic significance is more than enough reason to pay a visit to the church. The interior, too, of Leipzig's oldest church, which was founded in honour of St Nicholas, patron saint of merchants, holds interesting discoveries in store.

After the plain outside appearance, the bright interior comes as a surprise. It was designed in the late 18th century by Friedrich Dauthe with the refinements of the French Neoclassical style that was then fashionable, with green, white and pink stucco work, white pews and galleries, columns that sprout into palm trees and conceal the lower part of the Gothic cross-vault, and windows that are not visible from the nave. Paintings by Friedrich Oeser depicting scenes from the life of Christ complete the interior fittings.

The organ is a real gem. It has its origins in an instrument built by Friedrich Ladegast in 1862 for the specific purpose of playing organ music by Bach in the tradition of the 19th century. Today it is still the largest church organ in the state of Saxony.

Nikolaikirchhof

Gottfried Wilhelm Leibniz, Johann Gottfried Seume and Richard Wagner attended the Nikolaischule on the north side of the church, which was built in 1511–12 as a municipal school and served this purpose until the 19th century. In the historic class-

room on the ground floor, the tavern Alte Nikolaischule (➤ p. 42) is a good place to eat today. The first floor is a museum accommodating the university's collection of antiquities.

Nikolaikirchhof 2
♦ Tue–Thu, Sat–Sun
midday–5pm
www.uni-leipzig.de/
antik

Mädlerpassage

This tour finishes with a visit to one of the most magnificent arcades in the city. On the site of a trading house built in 1525 and named *Auerbachs Hof*, from 1912 the manufacturer Anton Mädler constructed a covered arcade, modelled on the Galleria Vittorio Emanuele II in Milan, which served as the basis for a four-storey trade fair house. Today the arcade has been restored to match the historic original, a gallery bathed in light. Its centre is an octagonal glass dome, beneath which a glockenspiel made of Meissen porcelain plays classical melodies and folk tunes at each full hour.

An advertising trick
According to the legend, Dr. Faustus came to the Easter fair at Leipzig with a few students and saw there how workmen were trying to raise a huge barrel from a wine cellar. When he remarked that a single person could carry it out on his own, the landlord promised him the entire contents of the barrel if he succeeded in doing this. Thereupon Faustus sat on the barrel and rode it out of the cellar – and his group made merry for three days on the marketplace. Because the story did not relate which wine cellar was the origin of these events, in 1625 the innkeeper Johann Vetzer commissioned Andreas Brettschneider to paint two panels depicting the scenes and backdated them by 100 years to the year when Auerbach's cellar was built.

More than anything the Mädlerpassage owes its fame to its cellar vaults, where Goethe spend a good deal of time while he was a student at Leipzig University. It was probably here that he heard the well-known legend of Dr Faustus riding a barrel, which he used in his drama *Faust* and thus made the story world famous. Statues of Faust and Mephisto on one side, and of bewitched drinkers on the other, lead down into the cellar, of which Goethe once wrote:

"Whoever travels to Leipzig to the fair, Without going to Auerbachs Hof, Should hold his tongue, as this proves, That he has not seen Leipzig."

»Have a break« [M3]
Enjoy Saxon specialities and a glass of wine in **Auerbachs Keller.**
♦ *noon–midnight*

17

Alma mater lipsiensis

... the name of the university where Leibniz, Goethe and Nietzsche, as well as Erich Kästner and Angela Merkel, were students, testifies to over 600 years of history. This seat of learning was founded in 1409 as a result of the Hussite movement in Prague and the migration of German students and professors from the Charles University there, and over the centuries it became one of the largest German universities. Today over 29,000 students are enrolled at

this classical full-range university, which covers the entire spectrum of subjects with its 14 faculties and 150 institutes and is scattered around the city at a number of sites.

www.zv.uni-leipzig.de

Augustusplatz

City-Hochhaus, Augustusplatz 9, www.panorama-leipzig.de

An assembly of a quite different kind took place over 20 years ago on the square at the eastern edge of the city centre, when 300,000 demonstrators chanted "We are the people". The 40,000-square-metre space named after the first king of Saxony was considered one of Germany's finest squares until the destruction of its Classical architecture in the Second World War. In 1968 GDR leader Walter Ulbricht's demolition teams finished it off by blowing up the late Gothic St Paul's Church and the Augusteum, both parts of the university, and the Gewandhaus.

The plan was to erect a socialist-style university on the square, then named after Karl Marx. The *City-Hochhaus*, a high-rise in the shape of an open book which was Germany's tallest building on completion in 1972, remains from this scheme. From the viewing terrace of the Panorama Tower at a height of 120 metres (9am-9pm) there is a wonderful city panorama. Since 2012, with the *Neues Augusteum*, the main building with the Auditorium Maximum and the *Paulinum* with its great hall and university church of St. Pauli, a modern building with historical references has replaced the historic university ensemble.

The building of light-coloured Elbe sandstone on the left is the opera house, which was inaugurated in 1960 with a performance of *The Meistersingers of*

Nuremberg. With a tradition going back over 300 years, the Leipzig opera is the third-oldest in Europe.

To see who commissioned the building take a look at the band of reliefs above the ground-floor windows, which depict theatrical symbols and state emblems of the GDR. The interior, with its brass handrails, wooden panelling, gold-leaf ornamentation, walls clad in Meissen porcelain and wine-red carpet, typifies the style of the late 1950s.

The home of the world-famous Leipzig *Gewandhaus* Orchestra is the concert hall opposite the opera. This concrete building of 1981 has a large glass façade that allows a view of the 714-square-metre and 31.80-metre-high mural *Gesang vom Leben (Song of Life)* by Sighard Gille. Inside the concert hall stairs lead to the Great Hall with its 1900

seats, which is renowned for its excellent acoustics.

The only element that has survived from the historic ensemble of Augustplatz is the magnificent fountain in front of the Gewandhaus, named *Mende-Brunnen* after the merchant's widow Pauline Mende († 1881) who donated it. Its theme is the importance of water to humankind. Marine creatures from Greek mythology surround an 18-metre obelisk, a design reminiscent of the famous Baroque fountains of Rome.

Gewandhaus Orchestra
City festivities once got their musical accompaniment from the three municipal horn blowers, but from 1743 an orchestra composed of 16 musicians took over. In that year prosperous merchants founded a concert society, the origin of one of the world's best-known symphony orchestras. It took its name from a concert hall in the house of the cloth merchants (➤ p. 14), its home from 1781. The Gewandhaus Orchestra has been a municipal institution since 1840, and is thus obliged to play on festive occasions and in the parish churches of St Thomas and St Nicholas. Many world premieres, guest appearances and tours, outstanding quality and renowned conductors such as Felix Mendelssohn Bartholdy (➤ p. 27), Kurt Masur and now Andris Nelson have brought international fame to what is the world's largest professional orchestra.

»Have a break« ⌂2
For a rest with a good view of Leipzig, go to the **Panorama Tower**.
Augustusplatz 9
◆ *Mon–Thu 11.30am–11pm, Fri–Sat 11.30am–midnight, Sun 9am–11pm*

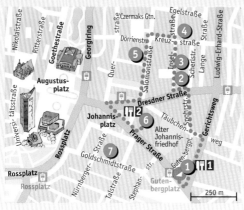

GRAPHICS QUARTER

1. Haus des Buches
2. Haus des Handwerks
3. Robert- und-Clara-Schumann-Museum
4. Reclam-Carrée
5. Brockhaus-Zentrum
6. Grassimuseum
7. Mendelssohn-Museum

[M]1 Literaturcafé
[M]2 Café in the Grassimuseum

SHOPPING ARCADES & GALLERIES

1. Barthels Hof
2. Webers Hof
3. Jägerhof
4. Kretschmanns Hof
5. Höfe am Brühl
6. Dussmann Passage
7. Steibs Hof
8. Oelßners Hof
9. Strohsackpassage
10. Theaterpassage
11. Specks Hof
12. Hansa Haus
13. Städtisches Kaufhaus
14. Dresdner Hof
15. Petersbogen mit Burgplatzpassage
16. Messehofpassage
17. Mädlerpassage
18. Königshauspassage
19. Marktgalerie
20. Handwerkerpassage

[M]3 Canito

Day 2

Cultural Walks

A City Stroll

Mus. d. Bild. Künste

3 Days in

Plagwitz

Strolling and Shopping

Battle of the Nations Monument

BATTLE OF THE NATIONS MONUMENT AND GRAPHICS QUARTER – MEMORIES

Today you will see a gigantic monument from inside before following in the footsteps of authors, booksellers and publishers in what was once Germany's foremost centre of the publishing business.

Battle of the Nations
A monument of this kind in Leipzig is in fact an astonishing sight, as the Saxons fought on side of the French. After the failure of Napoleon's Russian campaign of 1812, Tsar Alexander I, King Frederick William III of Prussia, Austria and Sweden formed an alliance against him with the support of Great Britain. With 361,000 men and 900 cannon, their army was twice as large as that of the French emperor and his allies. On 19 October 1813, after five days of fighting, Napoleon was so hard pressed that he had to flee to France. This was the beginning of the end of his domination of Europe. But at what a price: 120,000 soldiers lost their lives in this battle!

Völkerschlachtdenkmal
Prager Strasse/An der Tabaksmühle
▲ *Völkerschlachtdenkmal*
◆ *10am–6pm (April–Oct), 10am–4pm (Nov–March)*
www.stadtgeschichtliches-museum-leipzig.de

This colossal monument erected to commemorate the Battle of the Nations, which ended Napoleon's domination of Europe in 1813, is visible from afar. When the monument was initiated, it was intended as a celebration of a great victory, but by the time of its inauguration in 1913 on the eve of the First World War it was seen above all as a symbol of German strength. The city of Leipzig provided the land, and the construction costs of 6 million gold marks were financed by donations and the *League of German Patriots*.

Flanked by ramparts and gateways, which accommodate *ticket sales* in the east and Forum 1813 with a model of the battle in the west, the monument looms over a large pool of water, a *sea of tears* that symbolises the tears and the blood that were shed in the battle.

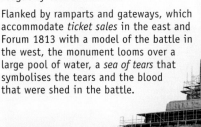

The patron saint of soldiers, the archangel Michael, stands guard at the foot of the monument below the inscription "God with us".

A lift leads to the *Hall of Fame*. Its crypt is a symbolic grave for the more than 120,000 soldiers who fell in the battle. Around a bronze tomb-cover set into the floor are double groups of stone soldiers behind death masks. Between the windows of the main floor, which takes the form of a gallery, four statues with a height of almost ten metres symbolise the virtues of the battle. They seem to be supporting the vault, whose dome is adorned with 324 almost life-size riders.

By climbing the 364 steps of a narrow spiral stair or taking the lift, visitors reach the observation terrace on the roof of the dome, where they have a wonderful view of Leipzig and its environs. The impressive monastery-like building in green surroundings is the crematorium in the middle of the south cemetery.

Tip: if you have the opportunity, go to a concert in the monument to the Battle of the Nations, as its acoustics are unique. Sounds echo back with a delay of some seconds, which makes classical choral music in this venue a remarkable experience.

(www.denkmalchor-leipzig.de)

Federal Administrative Court

Since 2002 the highest federal court for public law has once again had its seat in Leipzig, in one of the most beautiful palaces of justice in all of Europe. The domed building constructed in the 19th century as the Reichsgerichtsgebäude (imperial court of law), in which Karl Liebknecht among others was sentenced for high treason, served other purposes for decades, as a museum, geographical institute and recording studio, before being restored and returned to its original use. Today it is the seat of the Federal Administrative Court. Visitors can view the lobbies and principal courtroom and find out about the history of the building in the *Reichsgerichtsmuseum*.

Simsonplatz 1
▲ *Neues Rathaus*
◆ *Mon–Fri 8am–4pm*
www.bverwg.de

C.Bertelsmann

Book Fair

Every March more than 195,000 visitors come to Leipzig for four days to find out what is new on the book market. Leipzig Book Fair originated in the 17th century. Today it is the city's best-known fair, second only to the Frankfurt Book Fair for this business sector, and gives significant impulses to the book trade. The event is accompanied by the festival *Leipzig liest* (Leipzig reads), the award of the *Leipzig Book Fair Prize* and a *fair for second-hand books*.

www.leipziger-buchmesse.de

Graphics Quarter

Gutenbergstrasse is the starting point for a walk through the Graphisches Viertel, a quarter which before the Second World War was home to over 1000 bookstores, binders and printers, and more than 430 publishers, including renowned houses such as Baedeker, Brockhaus and Reclam. Much of the area was destroyed by bombing and a modest recovery in the GDR years ended with German reunification, so today the Graphics Quarter is a scene of 19th-century architecture alongside wasteland,

decayed buildings alongside prefabricated and modern blocks. However, these contrasts are what make the district so interesting: to this day signs of the renowned names of the past survive, leading visitors to many traces of the book city of old.

At the corner Prager Straße/Gerichtsweg a modern brick structure with glazed green courtyards on the site of the old house of booksellers' symbolises renewal. The large column of letters in front shows it to be the *Haus des Buches*, where exhibitions about books, readings and other events take place *(Gerichtsweg 28, www.haus-des-buches-leipzig.de)*.

Via Spohrstrasse, where there are lovely front gardens, the tour continues to Dresdner Strasse and

the *Haus des Handwerks*, a beautiful Art Nouveau building that was once the seat of Brandstetter, a printer of books and music.

At Inselstrasse no. 18 a fine Neoclassical house, its central section adorned with pilasters, takes you on a trip to Leipzig's musical past. Robert and Clara Schumann lived here for four years, and two of their eight children were born in the house, which now accommodates the *Robert-und-Clara-Schumann-Museum*. The world-famous Spring Symphony and the oratorio *Paradise* and *the Peri* were composed here. Visitors can see the historic rooms and attend readings and concerts in the Schumann Room *(Tue–Fri 2pm–6pm, Sat–Sun 10am–6pm, www.schumann-verein.de)*.

»Have a break«

Stop for a read in the **Literaturcafé** with its terrace and view of a lovely garden.

◆ *Mon–Fri 8am–3pm*

The stately yellow brick building on the next corner, the intersection with Kreuzstrasse, was once the seat of A.P. Reclam-Verlag, a publisher widely known for its "Universal Library", little yellow volumes of the classics of world literature. Today only the initials A.P.R. on the Art Nouveau main entrance serve as a reminder of those days. On the 19th-century building opposite, an unadorned plaque records that the *Kurt Wolff-Verlag*, publisher of a series called *Der jüngste Tag* (*Day of Judgement*), a platform for authors of the Expressionist period such as Kafka and Trakl, was based here.

Reclam's Universal Library

Generations of German pupils have used the books published by Reclam, little yellow volumes of the classics and modern works of world literature. As they are simply produced, they do not last long, but are cheap and suitable for making notes. They are part of the "Universal Library", which began on 10 November 1867 with Goethe's *Faust Part 1* as the first volume. The impulse was a decision of the federal assembly in 1856: from 9 November 1857 copyright for German authors was restricted to 30 years after their death, and their works could be published without payment of royalties from 1867. In this way the Leipzig publisher Reclam played a decisive part in bringing education to poorer sections of the population.

www.reclam.de

**The first
daily newspaper**
Something that is
taken for granted today
was published for the
first time in world
history in July 1650: a
daily newspaper called
the *Einkommende
Zeitungen*, consisting
of four pages in 13.5
x 17 cm format with
a circulation of 200
copies.

Its themes were
military campaigns
and international
commerce, trading
and court gossip, its
publishers were book-
sellers from Leipzig and
the printer Timotheus
Ritzsch. Since summer
1650 Ritzsch had is-
sued a newspaper four
times weekly. With its
10,000 inhabitants and
because of its trade
fairs, Leipzig was in
demand in those days
as a place where news
was exchanged. The
first printworks opened
here shortly after the
invention of printing.

Grassimuseum
Johannisplatz 5-11
▲ *Johannisplatz* ◆ *Tue–Sun 10am–6pm*
www.grassi-museum.de

At the end of the walk you come to an imposing
museum building, constructed in Expressionist
style of red porphyry tufa, with a golden pineapple
on its roof. When the museum was built in 1929,
St John's Church, then the site of Bach's sarcopha-
gus but destroyed in the war, stood in front of it,
which is why the decision was taken to restrict the
height of the museum.

Three large collections are housed in its various
wings, which means visitors have to allow plenty of
time or set priorities. The *Museum für Völkerkunde*,
founded in 1870 by citizens of Leipzig, is one
of Germany's largest ethnographic collections, a
journey to peoples and cultures in all parts of the
earth. If you want to know who the Andaman and
Nicobar peoples were, what is the significance of
a traditional souk in North Africa, how a teepee
appears from inside and what a shaman costume
of the Evenki looks like, or if you want to admire
the art of Benin, this is the place: every culture is
presented with its myths, traditions and adaptation
to the modern world.

Music fans go to the *Museum für Musikinstrumente*
of Leipzig University: from a Baroque trumpet to
a Renaissance lira da gamba, from a spinet to the

world's oldest fortepiano, both by the instrument maker Bartolomeo Cristofori – here you can learn everything about the world of musical instruments, immerse yourself in the history of Leipzig music and listen to compositions from the past.

For those who are more interested in interior design, the *Museum für Angewandte Kunst* (Museum of Applied Art) possesses well over 90,000 exhibits from all areas of crafts from antiquity to the present day. The particular strengths of the collection are Art Nouveau, Art Deco and Functionalism, as in those periods the museum was able to acquire its exhibits directly from samples shown at the trade fair. The annual highlight is the autumn fair named *Grassimesse*. Founded in 1920 as a *Modernist rendezvous*, since its revival in 1997 it has been an international forum for innovation and trends in applied art and product design.

(www.grassimesse.de)

Felix Mendelssohn Bartholdy (1809–47)

It is a short distance to the Neoclassical residence that houses the *Mendelssohn Museum*, where you can get an idea of how Felix Mendelssohn Bartholdy, composer and honorary citizen of Leipzig, lived and worked in the last years of his life. In addition to original furnishings, visitors can admire scores and manuscripts by the man who rediscovered the works of Johann Sebastian Bach, who became conductor of the Gewandhaus Orchestra at the age of just 28 and made it a world-famous ensemble, and who established Germany's first conservatory in Leipzig.

Goldschmidtstrasse 12
▲ *Rossplatz*
◆ *10am–6pm*
www.mendelssohn-stiftung.de

»Have a break« [m]2
For a rest after all the art, try the **Café** in the Grassi-museum!
Johannisplatz 5
◆ *Tue–Sun 10am–6pm*

ARCADES AND MORE – STROLLING AND WINDOW SHOPPING

Shopping is fun in Leipzig, whether you are in a historic trade fair building or a modern gallery, near the marketplace, in the railway station or on the KarLi.

"To the Venetians their bridges, to the Leipzigers their arcades": the pedestrian-friendly city centre is distinguished by its unique system of arcades and courtyards. They extend along the two main thoroughfares, Grimmaische Strasse und Petersstrasse, where the major fashion stores and department stores and the outlets of international retail chains attract window shoppers.

Before you head for the arcades, at the corner of Nikolaistrasse take a look at the oriel built of red porphyry: this copy of the *Fürstenhauserker* of 1538 is a reminder of one of the most beautiful Renaissance houses of the city, which took its name from four sons of noblemen who once lived here as students.

Here you are right next to *Specks Hof*, the oldest surviving arcade in the city with its three courtyards. It is connected to the *Hansa-Haus*, a trade fair building. Opposite Naschmarkt enter the *Mädler Passage* (➤ p. 21), which has a touch of Milanese flair with its mix of luxury shops and boutiques, and its continuation, the *Königshaus-* and *Messehofpassage*. *Petersbogen*, a modern arcade, links Petersstrasse with Burgplatz.

Christmas market
Each December visitors old and young come to Leipzig for specialities such as Pulsnitzer lebkuchen and glühwein, Christmas decorations from the Erzgebirge, the fairy-tale forest and concerts of wind instruments from the tower of the Altes Rathaus. 300 stands all round the marketplace have the old quarter as a historic backdrop. The great attractions include visits to Santa Claus and the world's largest free-standing Advent calendar. The Christmas market, one of the largest and most attractive in Germany, goes back to 1767.

www.leipzig.de/ weihnachtsmarkt

From Burgplatz you have a wonderful view of the *Neues Rathaus*, new city hall, one of the world's largest city halls with an area of about 10,000 square metres and almost 600 rooms.

Continue to the market-place, where the modern *Marktgalerie* fits in with the old system of passages. A little further on Hainstrasse note *Barthels Hof* (➤ p. 12), or go window shopping in the modern *Strohsack-Passage* on Nikolaistrasse, where you can see the largest clock in Europe that is set into the floor, and tell the time through a slab of glass while walking over it.

Within Europe's largest railway terminus is an extremely modern shopping centre: the 142 shops in the *Promenaden* open seven days a week to leave no wish unfulfilled *(Mon–Sat 9.30am–10pm, Sun 1pm–6pm)*.

Shopping is fun outside the city centre, too: *Gottschedstrasse* has many pubs and small but high-quality stores. For an alternative treat, cross the *KarLi*, a street south of the city centre named after Karl Liebknecht, a founder of the German Communist Party. The so-called *Löffelfamilie* ("spoon family") is a monument with a cult status in Leipzig: this lovingly restored neon advertisement by a GDR state-owned manufacturer of soup and tinned foods dates from 1973.

Ode to Joy

To find out where Schiller composed his Ode to Joy, take a trip to the north of Leipzig. In Gohlis, once a village, lies one of the city's oldest rustic houses, where Schiller stayed in 1785. Today it is a museum, the so-called Schillerhaus. Just round the

corner the Gohliser Schlösschen, built in Rococo style as a summer residence for Johann Caspar Richter, an alderman of the city, has an inviting restaurant and garden room.

Schillerhaus:
Menckestrasse 42
▲ *Menckestrasse*
♦ *Tue–Sun 10am–5pm (April–Oct),*
Wed-Sun 11am-4pm (Nov–March)
www.stadtgeschichtliches-museum-leipzig.de

Gohliser Schloss:
Menckestrasse 23
♦ *Restaurant:*
Mon-Sat from 11am,
Sat from 10 pm
www.gohliser-schloss.de

»Have a break« ⊓⅂3
Canito is a pleasant place to sample some antipasti and tapas!
Gottschedstrasse 13
♦ *Mon noon-3pm, Tue-Fri noon-midnight, Sat 3pm-midnight*

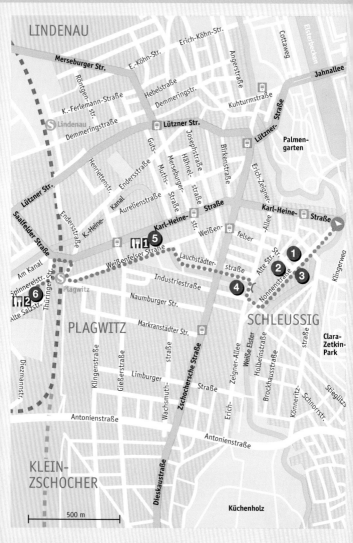

1 Museum of Printing

2 Elster-Business-Park

3 Buntgarnwerke

4 Riverboat

5 Stelzenhaus

6 Alte Baumwollspinnerei

1 Stelzenhaus

2 Café/Bistro in the Baumwollspinnerei

Day 3

The Art Scene

A City Stroll

Mus. d. Bild. Künste

3 Days in

Battle of the Nations Monument

Plagwitz

Strolling and Shopping

Ernst-Mey-Strasse
The name of a side street off Nonnenstrasse is a reminder of the man who is regarded as the founder of the mail-order business in Germany. In 1867 Carl Ernst Mey (1844–1903), a commercial counsellor for the Kingdom of Saxony, established a company to make paper collars and cuffs together with Bernhard Edlich, and moved it two years later from Paris to Plagwitz. Further branches were established in Leipzig, Berlin, Hamburg, London and Zurich, before Mey published his first illustrated mail-order catalogue in 1886 as a means of selling his products. This clever marketing ploy made him the number one in the world of mail order within just a few years!

PLAGWITZ – WATER, LOFTS AND ART

The morning is spent in the west of the city, where you can find out all about printing books, admire industrial architecture and charming back yards, take a walk along a canal and see Leipzig's best address for art.

Plagwitz
▲ *Nonnenstrasse*

Today it is difficult to imagine that Plagwitz was a little village up to the middle of the 19th century. In 1854 the lawyer Karl Heine purchased large areas of land, provided them with a modern infrastructure of roads, rail links and a waterway, and established textile mills, engineering factories and foundries here. This made Plagwitz the first industrial district in Leipzig.

An amazing variety of 19th-century industrial architecture can now be seen here – though it has been put to new uses. When their markets in eastern and central Europe collapsed after the end of communist rule, most production sites in Plagwitz were forced to close down. Their attractive buildings were restored, and soon became sought-after for use as apartments, studios, offices and business

premises thanks to their good transport links, location on a little river, the Weisser Elster, and beautiful lofts. Now an area of wonderful architecture with some picturesque back yards, little gardens and idyllic stretches of canal is waiting to be discovered. It is also possible to get a touch of Venetian atmosphere by viewing the scene from the water, as *Ristorante da Vito* operates trips in genuine gondolas from Venice! *(Nonnenstrasse 11, tel. 0341/4802626, www.da-vito-leipzig.de)*.

When technology got rolling

Veteran cars from over 100 years of motor history are exhibited in the former foundry of a factory for making ploughs and agricultural machines, later a state-owned producer. Veteran cars from England, America, Germany and the Czech Republic, polished and gleaming, and a great number of models dating from the 1920s to the 1950s are shown in the factory hall, now a mirrored event venue. They include Alfred Hitchcock's Buick Skylark Convertible, a Ford Model T, the first mass-produced car, and a Corvette. Tip: on Sundays from 10am to 2pm you can enjoy brunch in these unusual surroundings.

The first stop in Nonnenstrasse is an unusual museum where there is a smell of oil and printing ink in the air, and visitors are encouraged to join in for a hands-on experience. In the *Museum für Druckkunst* (Museum of Printing) you can learn about the art of printing books, using historic items such as hand presses, platen presses, lead type, wooden letters for type-setting by hand, machines for casting and setting type and a bookbinder's workshop. On weekdays you can also watch book printers, type setters and the last master of type-casting in Germany ply their trade, and even try it out for yourself.

(Nonnenstrasse 38, www.druckkunst-museum.de ◆ Mon–Fri 10am–5pm, Sun 11am–5pm)

Automuseum Da Capo Karl-Heine-Strasse 105 ◆ opening times see www.michaelis-leipzig.de

---

»Have a break«　🗺1

Cross the bridge to the other bank to get to **Restaurant Stelzenhaus**, where you can have a quick lunch.
Weissenfelser Strasse 65
◆ *Mon–Sat 11am–1am, Sun 9am–1am*

Leipzig School ...

... is the name given since the Documenta 6 exhibition at Kassel in 1977 to a current in representational painting. Its most prominent exponents are Bernhard Heisig, Wolfgang Mattheuer and Werner Tübke. As professors at the Leipziger Kunstakademie (Academy of Art) they influenced a whole generation of painters and graphic artists, and made Leipzig once again an internationally regarded centre for visual arts. Although they represent a considerable variety of styles, from Heisig's Expressionism to Mattheuer's New Objectivity and Tübke's Realism with surreal traits, what these painters of the 1970s and 1980s have in common are high artistic standards, an emphasis on craft skills, a representational but expressive approach combined with a "thoughtful, imaginative and profound interpretation of themes ranging from history to intimate areas of our environment".

The most striking complex is the red-brick building with light-coloured bands of stucco which extends on both sides of the river, connected by a gallery. Constructed in 1879 as the Sächsische Wollfabrik (Saxon wool factory), continually extended and made a state-owned business in the GDR period, the complex is today Europe's largest 19th-century industrial monument and has been used since renovation in the 1990s for residential, retail and commercial purposes. On the opposite side the *Elster Business Park* occupies what were once factory-owned apartments.

From Industriestrasse cross the Elisabethbrücke bridge to reach the 2.6-kilometre-long *Karl-Heine-Kanal*, which according to the plans of its eponymous builder was intended to connect the Weisser Elster with the Saale. Today a cycle and walking path runs here, which starts at the Kulturhafen Riverboat, an event location and a haven for Leipzig's creative people. Beyond the second bridge note the gigantic 1930s advertisement for Persil on a wall. Then it is possible to see from afar the red-brick building of the Verzinkerei Grohmann & Vroschen (galvanising works), known as the *Stelzenhaus* (*house on stilts*) because it projects over the water on tall concrete pillars. To end the walk here, take the path above the canal to Tschorrerstrasse and the Elsterpassage transport stop.

Alte Baumwollspinnerei
Spinnereistrasse 7
▲ *Train to Plagwitz,*
bus to Lindenau
www.spinnerei.de

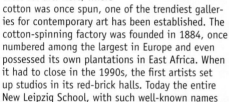

Weisenfelser Strasse leads to Leipzig's leading address for art. Here, where cotton was once spun, one of the trendiest galleries for contemporary art has been established. The cotton-spinning factory was founded in 1884, once numbered among the largest in Europe and even possessed its own plantations in East Africa. When it had to close in the 1990s, the first artists set up studios in its red-brick halls. Today the entire New Leipzig School, with such well-known names

as Neo Rauch, Tilo Baumgärtel, Julius Popp, Rosa Loy and Hans Aichinger, is represented in this former industrial complex. In the wake of the artists came the galleries, such as EIGEN + ART in the former hall for steam engines, then craft workers, designers, architects and the Residenz theatre and the LuRu cinema: an artists' colony where there are lots of exciting things to discover.

»Have a break« [m2]
The **Café Versorger** is an attractive place to while away some time, whether a delicious snack or just for coffee.
◆ *Mon–Fri from 8.30am,*
Sat 10am–6pm

Neue Leipziger Schule ...
... (New Leipzig School) denotes the third and fourth generations of a trend in modern art and has gained recognition as a label in

the art market. Works by Neo Rauch, the most prominent of the group, who produces surrealist works, Matthias Weischer, David Schnell and Tim Eitel are greatly sought-after by collectors and have become successful German exports. Essential impulses for their art came from Sighard Gille and Arno Rink, their professors at the Leipzig Hochschule für Grafik und Buchkunst (college of graphic and book art). It was above all the gallery-owner Gerd Harry Lybke who made Rauch known in the USA and in consequence brought other Leipzig artists into the international limelight.

MUSEUM DER BILDENDEN KÜNSTE – OLD AND NEW MASTERS

The cuboid building of glass and concrete on Sachsenplatz takes its visitors on a journey through art history. From Old Masters to the Barbizon painters and Leipzig School, from painting and sculpture to graphic art, photography and videos – the Museum der Bildenden Künste has many highlights.

Museum der Bildenden Künste

Katharinenstrasse 10
www.mdbk.de
▲ *Markt*
◆ *Tue, Thu–Sun 10am–6pm, Wed noon–8pm*

Naked, covered only with a cloak and with sandals on his feet as if he were an ancient god: Beethoven sits on a throne decorated with allegorical scenes, an eagle at his feet. Max Klinger used marble, onyx, ivory, precious stones and bronze in order to represent the composer, whose achievements elevated him to the world of the gods, in the pose of a heroic divinity. After 17 years Klinger presented this remarkable work to the public for the first time in 1902 on the occasion of the Vienna Secession exhibition. Later the Leipzig art museum bought the piece.

The colossal statue of Beethoven on the first floor is just one example of Klinger's oeuvre that can be admired here. Salome, Cassandra, Christ on Olympus and the Crucifixion of Christ: the city of Leipzig honours its famous son with a comprehensive show of his work.

Max Beckmann, born in Leipzig, is an equally strong presence in the museum.

Museum stories

The 35-metre-high modern cuboid of glass and concrete looks somewhat strange amidst its historic surroundings. Perhaps this is because only one of four L-shaped blocks planned as an architectural framework has been completed. The new building was inaugurated in 2004, but the history of the museum goes back to 1837, when Leipzig art lovers founded an art society. The society organised its first exhibition in 1848 at the Moritzbastei and gained its first museum building ten years later, on Augustusplatz. After damage at the hands of the Nazis and through bombing, the collection was housed for many years in the former court building, the Reichsgerichtsgebäude.

Art from 1900 to 1945 is presented in rooms adjoining the exhibition of Beckmann's works.

This is to mention only a small part of a collection that occupies a total of about 5,000 square metres and includes approximately 3,500 paintings, 1,000 sculptures and 60,000 sheets of drawings, prints and other graphic work. On four floors you can discover art from the late Middle Ages to the present day. Works by many famous painters, sculptors and

engravers are shown here – to name a small selection Lucas Cranach the Elder, Franz Hals, Rembrandt, Rubens, Tintoretto, Caspar David Friedrich, artists of the Barbizon School, Claude Monet, and Bernhard Heisig, Werner Tübke, Neo Rauch, Arne Rink and Tilo Baumgärtel as representatives of the Leipzig School.

The arrangement of the works is fascinating, as the presentation of the historic collection is accentuated by contemporary references. Although it seems that works from completely different worlds are placed together, unexpected juxtapositions open up different perspectives and lead to new points of view.

»Have a break« M3
Take time off from the art with coffee and cakes in the **Michaelis** in the Museum der Bildenden Künste.
♦ Tue, Thu–Sun 10am–6pm, Wed 10am–8pm

The *Self-Portrait with a Red Cap* ...
... depicts one of the leading GDR painters and most significant artists of the Leipzig School: Werner Tübke (1929–2004), professor and rector of the Hochschule für Grafik und Buchkunst (college of graphic and book art) in Leipzig. He became famous for one of the largest artistic projects of the 20th century, commissioned in 1976 by the GDR Ministry of Culture: a panorama in Bad Frankenhausen, 14 metres tall and 123 metres long, with the title *Early Bourgeois Revolution in Germany* (1983–1987, oil on canvas). It was intended to commemorate the Peasants' War and Thomas Müntzer. However, the result was not a battle painting, but a historical and philosophical visual cosmos of this era with over 3,000 different figures.

www.panorama-museum.de

37

Service

Hotels

In the city centre or near the trade fair, first-class hotel or design hotel: in Leipzig there are many good places to stay.

Leipzig Trade Fair

With about 35 fairs, including the Auto Mobil car show, the book fair and the industrial trade fair Intec, around 200 congresses, 9,400 exhibitors and 1,2 million visitors, the company Leipziger Messe GmbH is one of the ten largest organisers of trade shows in Germany. The eye-catching feature of the new fair with over 110,000 square metres of exhibition space is a spectacular lobby by the English star architect Ian Ritchie with 20,000 square metres of glass in its dome. Glazed bridges lead to the modern congress centre, which seats 10,000 visitors, and the five exhibition halls.

www.leipziger-messe.de

■ **art'otel leipzig city center******
Eutritzscher Strasse 15
04105 Leipzig (Mitte)
Tel. 0341/303840
Fax 0341/30384444
▲ Wilhelm-Liebknecht-Platz
www.artotel-leipzig.com

Modern art and design hotel with an ideal inner-city location.

■ **Victor's Residenz-Hotel Leipzig ******
Georgiring 13
04103 Leipzig (Mitte)
Tel. 0341/68660
Fax 0341/6866899
▲ Hauptbahnhof
www.victors.de

This elegant hotel with an Art Nouveau façade opposite the main station is the perfect base for all tourists and business travellers.

■ **Elster Lofts**
Nonnenstrasse 21
04229 Leipzig (Plagwitz)
Tel. 0341/21338800
Fax 0341/21338889
▲ Nonnenstrasse
www.apartment-leipzig.de

An alternative to a hotel: serviced loft apartments in a protected industrial landmark in Plagwitz, right on the waterfront and not far from the Clara-Zetkin-Park.

■ **Gästehaus Leipzig**
Wächterstrasse 32
04107 Leipzig (Mitte)
Tel. 0341/99990600
Fax 0341/99990601
▲ Neues Rathaus
www.gaestehaus-leipzig.de

A villa with its own park in an idyllic spot where once ministers and other guests of the city of Leipzig stayed, now extending a welcome to all guests.

■ **Galerie Hotel Leipziger Hof******
Hedwigstrasse 1-3
04315 Leipzig (Neustadt)
Tel. 0341/69740
Fax 0341/6974150
▲ Herrmann Liebmann-/ Eisenbahnstrasse
www.leipziger-hof.de

Comfortable private hotel in a lovely 19th-century house, a protected monument, with a remarkable art collection of over 200 works by famous Leipzig painters.

The Westin Leipzig

■ Hotel Fürstenhof*****
Tröndlinring 8
04105 Leipzig (Mitte)
Tel. 0341/1400
Fax 0341/1403700·
▲ Gördelerring
*www.hotelfuerstenhof
leipzig.com*

Leipzig's luxury hotel in a historic palais of 1770 on the edge of the city centre.

Lindner Hotel Leipzig

■ Hotel im Sachsenpark****
Walter-Köhn-Strasse 3
04356 Leipzig (Mockau-Nord)
Tel. 0341/52520
Fax 0341/5252528
▲ Messegelände
www.sachsenparkhotel.de

Business hotel directly opposite the trade fair and CCL, close to an 18-hole golf course.

■ Hotel Mercure Leipzig am Johannisplatz****
Stephanstrasse 6
04103 Leipzig (Mitte)
Tel. 0341/97790
Fax 0341/9779100
▲ Johannisplatz
www.mercure.com

Pleasant accommodation for business travellers and tourists, a few minutes' walk from the city centre.

■ Hotel Michaelis
Paul-Gruner-Strasse 44
04107 Leipzig (Südvorstadt)
Tel. 0341/26780
Fax 0341/2678100
www.hotel-michaelis.de

Privately run small hotel in a side street off the Karl-Lieb–knecht-Strasse entertainment district, near the city centre.

■ Leipzig Marriott Hotel****
Am Hallischen Tor 1
04109 Leipzig (Mitte)
Tel. 0341/96530
Fax 0341/9653999
▲ Hauptbahnhof
www.marriott.de

Modern luxury hotel near the railway station in the historic city centre, with a large spa.

Double M
The two superimposed blue Ms on the high-rise in Wintergarten-strasse at a height of 95 metres are Leipzig's best-known emblem. Designed in 1917 by

the Leipzig graphic artist Erich Gruner as a easily recognisable logo for the trade fair, the double M became world-famous within a very short time. The symbol derives from the sample fair (Mustermesse) which in 1895 replaced the goods fair – a world first. Instead of selling goods on the spot, samples were presented as a basis for traders to place an order and have the goods sent direct to their home address. Now the double M shines from the tower of the trade fair once again, but with a new meaning: Messen nach Mass (custom-made fairs).

Hotels

Elephant, tiger & co
This is the name of a documentary soap series which has made Leipzig Zoo known far beyond the city limits with its behind-the-scenes stories. The park-like zoo, founded in 1878 by an inn keeper named Ernst Pinkert as an attraction for his guests, is a zoo of the future. Its aim is to present animals in their natural habitats,

while taking visitors right around the world and covering 160 million years of earth's history. What this means can be seen in Pongoland, the world's largest enclosure for primates with an area of 30,000 square metres, the lion savannah Makasi Simba, the Gondwanaland, where you can go in search of the flora and fauna of the tropical rainforest, the Okapi Forest and the Ganesha Mandir elephant compound.

Pfaffendorfer Strasse 29
Tel. 0341/5933500
www.zoo-leipzig.de
▲ *Zoo*
◆ *April, Oct 9am–6pm,*
May–Sept 9am–7pm,
Nov–March 9am–5pm

■ **Lindner Hotel Leipzig****
Hans-Driesch-Strasse 27
04179 Leipzig (Leutzsch)
Tel. 0341/44780
Fax 0341/4478478
▲ Rathaus Leutzsch
www.lindner.de

Modern hotel for business and sports in Leutzsch, a high-quality residential district. Close to the Auenwald, free airport shuttle service.

■ **Motel One Leipzig**
Nikolaistrasse 23
04109 Leipzig (Mitte)
Tel. 0341/3374370
Fax 0341/33743710
▲ Hauptbahnhof
www.motel-one.com

Reasonably priced design hotel in the pedestrian zone opposite the Nikolaikirche.

■ **NH Leipzig Messe****
Fuggerstrasse 2
04158 Leipzig (Mockau-Nord)
Tel. 0341/52510
Fax 0341/5251300
▲ Neue Messe
www.nh-hotels.de

Modern conference and business hotel with a spa at the trade fair grounds.

■ **Park Hotel Leipzig****
Richard-Wagner-Strasse 7
04109 Leipzig (Mitte)
Tel. 0341/98520
Fax 0341/9852750
▲ Hauptbahnhof
www.parkhotelleipzig.de

Behind the protected Art Nouveau façade of the former Grand Hotel opposite the station there is today a first-class hotel in Art Deco style.

Gästehaus Leipzig

■ **pentahotel Leipzig**
Grosser Brockhaus 3
04103 Leipzig (Mitte)
Tel. 0341/1292760
Fax 0341/1292800
▲ Johannisplatz
www.pentahotels.com

Flatscreen TVs, wifi, rain showerheads, marble bathrooms and a lounge designed by Matteo Thun: all of this makes the Penta in the Graphics Quarter near the city centre a new breed of hotel.

■ **Quartier M**
Markgrafenstrasse 10
04109 Leipzig (Mitte)
Tel. 0341/21338800
Fax 0341/21338889
▲ Wilhelm-Leuschner-Platz, Neues Rathaus
www.apartment-leipzig.de

Modern apartments in a historic residence at the edge of the Johanna-Park.

■ **Radisson Blu Hotel Leipzig****⁺**
Augustusplatz 5-6
04109 Leipzig (Mitte)
Tel. 0341/21460
Fax 0341/2146815
▲ Augustusplatz
www.radissonblu.com

Elegant hotel behind a glass façade with a direct view of the opera house and Gewandhaus.

■ **Ramada Hotel Leipzig****
Schongauer Strasse 39 (Paunsdorf)
04329 Leipzig
Tel. 0341/2540
Fax 0341/2541550
▲ Paunsdorf Center
www.h-hotels.com

Large conference hotel near the trade fair grounds.

■ **The Westin Leipzig****
Gerberstrasse 15
04105 Leipzig (Mitte)
Tel. 0341/9880
Fax 0341/9881229
▲ Hauptbahnhof
www.westin-leipzig.com

Centrally located five-star hotel, the largest conference hotel in Leipzig, distinguished by a high standard of helpful service.

In composers' footsteps

If you would like to follow the trail of great composers and 800 years of music history in Leipzig, look out for the curving ribbon of stainless steel set into the ground in the city centre. It is part of the Leipziger Notenspur, the "Leipzig trail of notes" connecting the places where musicians and composers such as Telemann, Bach, Mendelssohn, Schumann,

Wagner, Grieg, Mahler and Reger lived and worked, and leads from the Gewandhaus to the Opera, the Paulinum and the MDR Cube. So that the music can be heard, there are sound installations at all 23 stations. With this globally important cultural heritage, Leipzig is applying for inclusion in the German list of proposals for UNESCO World Heritage.

www.notenspur-leipzig.de

Cafés and Lunch

At lunchtime you have to make a difficult choice: the culinary offerings in the city centre range from Leipziger Lerche and other delicious pastries to Saxon food and crossover.

Leipzig Calendar

January
★ Partner Pferd:
www.partner-pferd.de

March
★ Bookfair:
www.leipziger-buchmesse.de
★ Jazz festival for new talents:
www.facebook.com/pg/jazznachwuchsfestival

April
★ Frühjahrs-Kleinmesse:
www.leipziger-kleinmesse.net
★ Historical Easter fair:
www.heureka-leipzig.de
★ Leipzig Marathon:
www.leipzigmarathon.de

May
★ Museum night:
www.museumsnacht-halle-leipzig.de
★ Soap box car race:
www.seifenkiste.nato-leipzig.de

June
★ Bachfest:
www.bachfestleipzig.de
★ City festival:
www.leipzigerstadtfest.de
★ Wagner festival:
www.wagner-verband-leipzig.de

■ **Café Corso**
Brüderstrasse 6 (Mitte-Süd)
▲ Rossplatz
◆ Mon–Fri 8am–6pm, Sat 10am–5pm

A traditional Leipzig patisserie. Come here to try Baumkuchen, Leipziger Lerchen, Christstollen or one of many other delicious specialities.

■ **Café Grundmann**
August-Bebel-Strasse 2 (Südvorstadt)
▲ Engelsdorf, Gymnasium
◆ Mon-Fri 8am-11pm, Sat 9am-11pm, Sun 9am-7pm

The last authentic "Viennese café" in the southern district of Leipzig with a 1930s atmosphere. As well as tempting cakes they serve lunches and cocktails.

■ **Café Kandler**
Thomaskirchhof 11 (Mitte)
▲ Thomaskirche
◆ 10am–8pm

One of Leipzig's finest addresses for cream gateaux and other cakes.

■ **Caffe Pascucci**
Thomasgasse 2-4 (Mitte)
▲ Augustusplatz
◆ Mon–Sat from 8am

Here you can drink your way through the world's blends of coffee, accompanied by cake, ice cream and pasta.

■ **Eisdiele Pfeifer**
Kochstrasse 20 (Südvorstadt)
▲ Südplatz
◆ Mon-Fri noon-6 pm, Sat-Sun 1-6 pm

An ice-cream salon where the clock seems to have stopped in the year 1953. The home-made ice cream still tastes incredibly good, just as it did back then!

■ **Kaffeehaus Riquet**
Schuhmachergässchen 1 (Mitte)
▲ Markt
◆ 9am–7pm

This well-known Art Nouveau building with elephants' heads is an old-style coffee house: waitresses in starched white aprons serve delicious cakes and speciality coffees.

■ **Kafic**
Karl-Tauchnitz-Strasse 9-11 (Mitte-Süd)
▲ Robert-Schumann-Strasse
◆ Mon–Sat 10am–midnight, Sun 10am–7pm

Café in the Galerie für Zeitgenössische Kunst, a meeting place for various cultures.

■ **Maitre**
Karl-Liebknecht-Strasse 62 (Südvorstadt)
▲ Südplatz
◆ Mon–Fri 8am–midnight, Sat 9am–midnight, Sun 9am–10pm

A coffeehouse in wonderful

Art Nouveau surroundings with a patisserie attached.

■ **Sakura - Kaiten Sushi Bar**
Bosestrasse 4 (Mitte-West)
▲ Gottschedstrasse
◆ Mon–Fri 11.30am–2.30pm, Mon–Sun 6pm–midnight

Recommended for all lovers of raw fish!

■ **Schiller**
Schillerstrasse 3 (Mitte)
▲ Wilhelm-Leuschner-Platz
◆ Tue–Wed 5pm-11pm
Thu–Sat 11.30am-midnight

This place is all about seeing and being seen. But it is also worth coming for the food – from zurek, a Polish cabbage soup, to duck liver paté and braised calf's cheek.

■ **Telegraph**
Dittrichring 18-20 (Mitte)
▲ Goerdelerring
◆ Mon–Fri from 8am, Sat-Sun from 9am

Whether you feel like a late breakfast or a hot meal, Telegraph is a wonderful place at any time of day.

■ **Zill's Tunnel**
Barfussgässchen 9
▲ Markt
◆ 11.30am–midnight

All those with a taste for Saxon food should eat a meal at this authentic inn.

Leipzig Calendar

★ Wave-Gotik-Meet:
www.wave-gotik-treffen.de

July
★ Sommer-Kleinmesse:
www.leipziger-kleinmesse.net
Weinfest: *www.leipzig.de*

August
★ Classic Open:
www.classicopenleipzig.de
★ Water festival:
www.wasserfest-leipzig.de

September
★ Herbst-Kleinmesse:
www.leipziger-kleinmesse.net
★ Mendelssohn festival:
www.mendelssohn-stiftung.de
★ Schumann week:
www.schumann-verein.de

October
★ Grassimesse:
www.grassimesse.de
★ Jazz days:
www.jazzclub-leipzig.de/jazztage/
★ Lachmesse (comedy festival):
lachmesseleipzig.wordpress.com

November
★ euro-scene, Festival zeitgenössischen europäischen Theaters und Tanzes:
www.euro-scene.de
★ International Leipzig festival for documentary and animated film:
www.dok-leipzig.de

December
★ Christmas market:
www.leipzig.de

Restaurants

From gourmet restaurants to little tapas bars, the culinary scene in Leipzig has everything the heart could desire!

Leipzig's vital statistics

Leipzig is situated in the north-west of the Free State of Saxony. With a population of 570,000, it is the biggest city in the five new federal states (former GDR). About 30,000 residents are not of German nationality.

The municipality of Leipzig covers an area of almost 300 square kilometres. More than one third of this is used for agriculture, and almost 15 per cent consists of woodland and green spaces. The population density is 1,733 persons per square kilometre.

Leipzig lies on the north German plain. The Weisser Elster river flows through it and into the Pleisse and Parthe. The city boundary is almost 129 kilometres long; the maximum extent of the city is 23.4 kilometres north-south, and 21.3 kilometres east-west. Its highest point is 113 metres above sea level, its lowest 98 metres.

■ **Bacco 36**
Waldstrasse 36 (Mitte)
Tel. 01 77/6 892427
▲ Waldplatz
◆ Tue-Sat 9am-10pm,
Sun 9am-9pm

A well-conceived mixture of delicatessen and trattoria, where antipasti, fresh panini and pasta are to be had.

■ **Barthels Hof**
Hainstrasse 1 (Mitte)
Tel. 0341/141310
▲ Markt
◆ Mon-Sat 11.30am-11pm,
Sun 10am-11pm

Fine regional specialities and more await diners in the last surviving Baroque passage courtyard in Leipzig.

■ **C'est la vie**
Zentralstrasse 7 (Mitte)
Tel. 0341/97501210
▲ Thomaskirche
◆ Tue-Sat 6pm-midnight
www.cest-la-vie.restaurant

If you like to eat fine French cuisine and love foie gras, fish and crustaceans, this is the place to come.

■ **Chinabrenner**
Giesserstrasse 18 (Plagwitz)
Tel. 0341/2409102
▲ Naumburger Strasse,
Markranstädter Strasse
◆ Mon 12 noon-3pm, Tue-Sat 12 noon-11pm

In what was once the metal foundry of the Kirow-Werke, Thomas Wrobel cooks delicious meals from the food stalls of the Chinese province of Sichuan.

■ **Falco Restaurant**
Gerberstrasse 15 (in the Westin Hotel/Mitte-Nord)
Tel. 0341/9882727
▲ Wilhelm-Liebknecht-Platz
◆ Tue-Sat 6pm-10pm

Michelin-starred restaurant on the 27th floor of the Westin Hotel, with a breathtaking view to complement duck liver paté, scallops and other treats.

Gourmet Restaurant Falco

Niemanns Tresor

■ La Cosita
Karl-Liebknecht-Strasse 89
(Mitte-Süd)
Tel. 0341/3038246
▲ Südplatz
◆ Mon–Fri 11.30am-3pm,
from 5 pm, Sat-Sun from
11.30am

Caribbean atmosphere
on the KarLi: indulge in
dreams of holidays while
eating rollos, camarones
à la Habana, salsa picante
and other Latin American
delicacies.

■ Panorama Tower
29th floor, City-Hochhaus
Augustusplatz 9 (Mitte)
Tel. 0341/7100590
▲ Augustusplatz
◆ Mon–Thu 11.30am-11pm,
Fri-Sat 11.30am-midnight,
Sun 9am-11pm

High above the rooftops
of Leipzig, a restaurant in
four parts – Tokyo, Cape
Town, New York and St
Petersburg – provides not
only a panoramic view of
the city, but also tasty
crossover cuisine.

■ Passion
Möckernsche Strasse 21
(Gohlis-Süd)
Tel. 0341/5503745
▲ Wideritzscher Strasse
◆ Tue–Fri 11.30am–2pm,
Tue–Sat 6pm–midnight

Mediterranean feeling in
Gohlis with outstanding
German food.

■ Schaarschmidts
Coppistrasse (Gohlis)
Tel. 0341/9120517
▲Virchowstrasse/
Coppistrasse
◆ Mon–Sat 5pm–midnight,
Sun noon–midnight

Leipzig's leading address
for high-class cooking, and
unusual creative dishes.

■ Stadtpfeiffer Restaurant im Gewandhaus
Augustusplatz 8 (Mitte)
Tel. 0341/2178920
▲ Augustusplatz
◆ Tue–Sat from 6pm

A well-known gourmet
destination in the Gewandhaus, appealing to all the
senses.

■ Herrenhaus Möckern
Bucksdorffstraße 43
(Möckern)
Tel. 0341/91878387
▲ Slevogtstraße,
Möckern, Hist. Straßen-
bahnhof
◆ Tue-Sat from 6.30pm

Whether you enjoy
Peter Niemann´s aromatic
cooking in the gourmet
restaurant Residenz or
the down-to-earth
German food in Brennerei,
it is well worth making
the trip out to the north
of Leipzig.

■ Weinwirtschaft
Thomaskirchhof 13-14
(Mitte)
Tel. 0341/496141
▲ Goerdelerring
◆ 7am-11pm

Popular haunt of visitors
and locals, with tapas
and classic regional and
Mediterranean dishes on
the menu.

At 205 metres the tallest
structure in Leipzig is the
chimney of the *Bösdorf
steelworks* in the district
of Knautnaundorf. It is
followed by the DVB-T
transmission mast in
Connewitz at 190 metres
and the City-Hochhaus
on Augustusplatz at
142.5 metres.

With the neighbouring
city of Halle, Leipzig
is part of the Sachsen-
dreieck (Saxon Triangle)
metropolitan region. Its
central location makes it
a hub of transport and
logistics, a gateway for
the east to the markets
of Europe, for the west
to the new EU countries
in eastern Europe. Once
a major industrial centre,
Leipzig has attracted
such renowned compa-
nies as BMW, Porsche and
Siemens, and enterprises
of the communications
and information technol-
ogy sectors have made it
their base.

As an old trading city,
Leipzig has a modern
trade fair and congress
centre, and is among the
top congress cities in
Germany. It is the site
of several high-ranking
research institutes, and
about 36,000 students
are enrolled at its seven
universities and colleges.
Leipzig is a popular
destination for city trips,
with more than 2,9 mil-
lion overnight stays, and
has an excellent tourist
infrastructure with its
more than 15,000 beds
for guests.

Pubs and Beer Gardens

Whether you feel like gose, the local beer speciality, or vodka, or want a dance in a pub or beer garden, Leipzig has something for every taste.

Leipziger Allerlei ...

... (Leipzig allsorts) consists of young vegetables such as carrots, peas, asparagus and morels, but can also include kohlrabi, beans or cauliflower, and is served with boiled crayfish. Today a delicacy, it was invented in times of need: after the Napoleonic wars Leipzig was a prosperous city, and wanted to keep out beggars and tax collectors. A town scribe therefore recommended the city councillors to conceal all expensive ingredients such as morels or meat beneath the vegetables, and to garnish the meal with nothing more than a small crayfish from the river Pleisse. Guests from elsewhere were served only what was on top, so that they got only vegetables, and thus the beggars and tax collectors were happy to move on to some other place.

■ Bayerischer Bahnhof
Bayrischer Platz 1 (Mitte-Süd)
▲ Bayrischer Platz
◆ 11-midnight

An inn and gose brewery in the world's oldest railway terminus, where you can
try a variety of gose creations.

Spizz Jazz & Musikclub

■ Café Luise
Bosestrasse 4 (Mitte-West)
▲ Gottschedstrasse
◆ from 9am

A great place for breakfast, a quick lunch or a cocktail, Café Luise is a good choice
at any time of day.

■ Glashaus
Clara-Zetkin-Park (Mitte-Süd)
▲ Clara-Zetkin-Park
◆ Wed-Sun 9am-9pm

This popular rendezvous in the middle of the park is like a little bit of holiday.

■ Gosenschenke
Ohne Bedenken
Menckestrasse 5 (Gohlis)
▲ Fritz-Seger-Strasse
◆ from noon

A historic gose tavern, where you can try this special Leipzig beer in a well-frequented inn with a lovely beer garden beneath spreading old trees.

■ Killiwilly
Karl-Liebknecht-Str. 44 (Südvorstadt)
▲ Südplatz
◆ Sun-Tue 10am-3am, Wed 10am-4am, Thu 10am-5am, Fri-Sat 10am-7am

A cosy pub serving Guinness, Kilkenny and cider on draught with pleasant outdoor seating, a place to watch football and have a party.

■ LuLu Lottenstein
Karl-Liebknecht-Str. 63 (Südvorstadt)
▲ Südplatz
◆ from 10am

Attractive pub and restaurant, where modern works by the artist Lulu Lottenstein adorn the walls.

Mückenschlösschen
Waldstrasse 86
(Mitte-Nordwest)
▲ Waldplatz
◆ 11am–midnight

A great place for an excursion, not just in summer: a restaurant and beer garden in historic surroundings right by the entrance to the Waldstrassenviertel.

Puschkin
Karl-Liebknecht-Strasse 74
(Südvorstadt)
▲ Südplatz
◆ 9am-2am

An in-place on the KarLi, open for guests at any time of day.

Spizz Jazz & Musicclub
Markt 9 (Mitte)
▲ Markt
◆ from 9am
Club programme at
www.spizz.org

Hungry guests eat here with a view of the marketplace, while down below the cellar is for jazz – or soul and funk.
A jazz funk disco and piano boogie night, as well as concerts and readings, feature regularly on the programme.

Vinothek 1770
Tröndlinring 8 (Mitte)
▲ Goerdelerring
◆ from noon

For those who like a high-class ambience, the wine bar in the Fürstenhof luxury hotel is just the place. 170 fine wines are on offer here.

Vodkaria
Gottschedstrasse 15
(Mitte-West)
▲ Gottschedstrasse
◆ from 5pm

Guests in this atmospheric bar can look forward to more than 400 sorts of vodka, almost 100 cocktails and dishes from the vodka belt that spans Poland, Russia and the way to Scandinavia.

Volkshaus
Karl-Liebknecht-Strasse 32
(Südvorstadt)
▲ Südplatz
◆ from 9.30am

For a glass of wine or a cigar, for flammkuchen (speciality of Alsace) or a party, the Volkshaus attracts a wide range of guests.

Leipziger Lerche
... ("Leipzig lark") is a little cake of shortcrust pastry filled with almonds, nuts and jam, and decorated with two crossed strips of dough. This delightful pastry filled a gap: in the 18th and 19th centuries songbirds really were caught in Leipzig and prepared for the table in many different ways. Larks were a delicacy – over 400,000 of them are said to have been sold in one single year, 1720. When there was a danger that larks would be extinct in the Leipzig region in the 19th century, the king of Saxony banned

catching them in 1876. Thus today only a little cake remains, with two crossed strips of pastry as a reminder of the strings that were once wrapped around a stuffed lark.

Bars & Nightlife

If you want to dance the night away in Leipzig or just chill out over a cocktail, all you have to do is read on ...

The Moritzbastei ...

..., MB for short, and famous as the largest student club in Europe, is a cultural centre today and has become one of the best-known nightspots in Leipzig. The old walls of a bastion that Hierony-mus Lotter built for Prince Elector Moritz of Saxony between 1551 and 1554 as part of the city defences later ac-commodated a citizens' school and then from the 1970s a student club. After the peaceful revolution of 1989 the Moritzbastei became a limited company owned by the university foundation. There is always something going on here: with a café, brick terrace, wine bar and pub the old bastion is a popular place to meet, and its wide-ranging programme extends to concerts, exhibitions, films and parties.

www.moritzbastei.de

■ BarCelona
Gottschedstrasse 12 (Mitte-West)
▲ Gottschedstrasse
◆ Mon–Sat from 5pm, Sun from 9am

A little bit of Spain in Leipzig: a tapas bar with a nice beer garden.

■ Bar „Wintergarten" im Hotel Fürstenhof
Tröndlinring 8 (Mitte)
▲ Goerdelerring
◆ from noon

For five o'clock tea or a cocktail, you can in the winter gardenof the Fürstenhof Hotel.

■ Bricks
Brühl 52 (Mitte)
▲ Hauptbahnhof
◆ 8pm–5am

Cellar bar in eighties style, where the bar staff are consummate masters of the art of mixing a cocktail.

■ Chocolate Leipzig
Gottschedstrasse 1 (Mitte-West)
▲ Gottschedstrasse
◆ from 5pm

A hip location with a beautiful brick interior.

On Wednesday the house band Max Express plays live music to go with your long drinks.

■ Elsterartig
Dittrichring 17 (Mitte)
▲ Thomaskirche
◆ Tue-Sa from 6pm

For eating a burger, dancing or partying, the club is a new hotspot in Leipzig's nightlife.

■ Falco Bar & Lounge
Gerberstrasse 15 (in the Westin Hotel/Mitte-Nord)
▲ Hauptbahnhof
◆ Tue-Sat from 6pm

Pleasant surroundings to finish the evening with a nightcap: enjoy cohina and whisky (or whatever your tipple is) while Leipzig by night lies at your feet.

Volkspalast

Gose ...

... is a top-fermented beer that gets its characteristic, slightly sour taste from the addition of cooking salt and coriander and from a generous amount of biological lactic acid. According to legend Emperor Otto III drank this beer a thousand years ago in the town of Goslar, where it got its name from the little river Gose, which flows from the Harz mountains. The first written reference dates from 1332, at the monastery of Ilsenburg, from where the beer spread.

In 1738 Prince Leopold I of Anhalt-

■ **Kleine Träumerei**
Münzgasse 7 (Südvorstadt)
▲ Hohe Strasse/LVB
◆ Mon–Sat from 7pm

A small café-bar-lounge serving snacks, and a relaxing place for a cocktail: the name means "dreaming a little".

Kleine Träumerei

■ **La Playa Beach Club**
Altes Messegelände (Probstheida)
▲ An den Tierkliniken, Altes Messegelände
◆ from noon (May-Sept.)
www.beach-club-leipzig.de

Get the genuine Caribbean feeling at the old trade-fair site: cocktails, beach ball or party, there is always some action here.

■ **Nachtcafe**
Petersstrasse 39-41
▲ Wilhelm-Leuschner-Platz
◆ Wed, Fri-Sat 10pm–5am

Come here on the Energy Clubnight or Energy Glory Night, and dance the hours away.

■ **Rudi Bar**
Merseburger Strasse 48 (Lindenau)
Tel. 0177/4307205
▲ Lützner/Merseburger Strasse
◆ Mon-Sat 6pm-3am
www.rudi-bar.de

A hip bar, a meeting place for the artistic and intellectual Boheme of west Leipzig, among others.

■ **Sol y Mar**
Gottschedstrasse 4 (Mitte-West)
▲ Gottschedstrasse
◆ from 9am

An oasis of indulgence in the city centre: take your shoes off and put your feet up: the Balinese furnishings are incredibly relaxing for a cocktail and, if you want, a massage.

■ **Spagos Lounge im Radisson Blu Hotel Leipzig**
Augustusplatz 5-6 (Mitte)
▲ Augustusplatz
◆ from 10.30am

For an aperitif or digestif, pass a quiet hour in the leather sofas of this elegant bar on Augustusplatz.

Gosenschenke Ohne Bedenken

Dessau is said to have brought the beer to Leipzig, where it was produced up to the 1960s. In 1986 the tavern named Ohne Bedenken (*no worries*) was the first to serve this Leipzig speciality once again, and the beer can now be found on many menus.

49

Wellness

If you want to recuperate from everyday stress or just to let your soul float free, in Leipzig you will find every kind of treatment from massage to shiatsu and saunas.

Pier1

Cospudener See

Just half an hour from the city centre is where holidays begin: on the south side of Leipzig, at its border with Markkleeberg, where once huge excavators dug lignite from the earth, an area of lakes – no less than 15 of them – is emerging. One of the most popular lakes in this district, known as *Neuseenland* (*New Sealand*), is the Cospudener See, where beaches of fine-grained sand attract swimmers and sunbathers in summer. Rowing, surfing, sailing and angling go on all year, cyclists and inline skaters make the circuit of the lake, and hiking paths are an invitation to see the neighbouring villages.

www.leipzigseen.de

■ **Entspannwerk**
Breslauer Strasse 32
(Stötteritz)
tel. 0341/8605722
▲ Weißestrasse
◆ Mon–Fri 9am-8pm,
Sat 9am-2pm

Here you can treat yourself to many different cosmetic and wellness treatments.

The Westin Leipzig

■ **Finnlandsauna am Baggersee**
Kiebitzstrasse 20 (Thekla)
▲ Samuel-Lampel-Strasse
◆ 10-22 Uhr
www.finnlandsaunaambaggersee.de

A varied sauna landscape where you can lie on the lawn between sweat sessions, relax in the pool or the bio-bath, or get fit with aqua-gymnastics.

■ **Grünauer Welle**
Stuttgarter Allee 7
(Grünau)
▲ Stuttgarter Allee
◆ Tue, Thu noon–10pm,
Wed 8am–10pm, Fri noon-
3pm, Sat 10am–9pm,
Sun 10am–6pm
www.sportbaeder-leipzig.de

Sauna fans will find Finnish, steam and bio-sauna here, as well as a swimming pool.

■ **Hotel Fürstenhof**
Tröndlinring 8 (Mitte)
▲ Gördelerring
◆ Mon–Fri 6.30am–10pm,
Sun till 10pm (summer)
www.hotelfuerstenhof leipzig.com

Enjoy the luxury of a five-star hotel and indulge yourself in the AquaMarin Spa with pools, Finnish sauna, Roman steam bath, a range of massages and a gym for working out.

■ **Ökobad Lindenthal**
Am Freibad 3 (Lindenthal)
▲ Lindenthaler Hauptstrasse
www.sportbaeder-leipzig.de

Leipzig's natural swimming pool with an ecological

LaLita

pond, a biotope for plants and animals as well as recreation.

■ **Sachsen Therme**
Schongauer Strasse 19 (Paunsdorf)
▲ Sommerfeld
◆ 10am–11pm
www.sachsen-therme.de

Forget your daily cares for a few hours at this 18,000-square-metre spa with its pools, saunas and gym facilities.

■ **Sauna im See**
Hafenstrasse 19 (Markkleeberg)
▲ Zöbigker, Schmiede
◆ Mon 11am–10pm, Tue–Sun 10am–10pm
www.sauna-im-see.de

This is no run-of-the-mill sauna: after having a good sweat you can dive straight into the crystal-clear water of the Cospudener See and enjoy a wide-ranging view of the lake and harbour on the terrace or from behind the big terrace windows.

■ **Sawadee**
Gottschedstrasse 6 (Mitte-West)
▲ Gottschedstrasse
◆ Mon–Sat noon–9pm
www.sawadee-wellnessmassagen.de

Many kinds of massage are on offer here – from Thai and hot stone to foot reflexology and shiatsu – to ease both body and soul.

■ **Sportbad an der Elster**
Antonienstrasse 8 (Kleinzschocher)
▲ Rödelstraße, Adler
◆ Mon–Thu 2-10pm, Fri 8am-9pm, Sat 11am-4pm, Sun 8am-4pm (Thu women only)
www.sportbaeder-leipzig.de

Here you can both swim and have a sauna.

■ **Wellness Oase Paradies**
Kochstrasse 138 (Connewitz)
Tel. 0341/3068934
▲ Connewitz Kreuz
◆ Mon–Thu 9am–9pm, Fri 9am–6pm
www.wellness-oase-paradies.de

Come here to treat yourself and your skin!

■ **Work Fit**
Trufanowstrasse 10 (Gohlis)
▲ Chausseehaus
Reservations: tel. 0341/5204745
www.work-fit.de

This holistic massage practice relieves your tensions with TouchLife and Ayurveda massage and Medi Akupress.

Culture

Alongside Bach and Mendelssohn, the Gewandhaus Orchestra and the Tho¬manerchor, Leipzig's cultural scene offers top-class theatre, lots of cabaret, cinema and literature.

Thomaner ...

... is the name for choirboys who sing in the famous choir that was founded in 1212 together with St Thomas' Church (Thomaskirche) and its school, the Thomasschule. The approximately 100 members of the choir live according to strict rules in a boarding school, and have been directed over the centuries by many well-known musicians and composers – including Johann Sebastian Bach, whose cantatas, motets and longer choral works are particularly important to the choir, even though their repertoire spans the range from Gregorian chants to modern compositions. Since the 1920s, when the choir made its first tour abroad under its cantor Karl Straube, the Thomaner have regularly travelled for their concerts. In Leipzig itself the boys can be heard singing at Sunday service and for the weekly motets.

www.thomanerchor.de

Music

■ **Bach-Archiv Leipzig**
Thomaskirchhof 16 (Mitte)
▲ Thomaskirche
Tel. 0341/91370
Programme at
www.bach-leipzig.de

Varied concerts connected with Bach in St Thomas' Church, the Bosehaus, Altes Rathaus, Mendelssohn-Haus etc.

HOCHSCHULE FÜR MUSIK UND THEATER
Felix Mendelssohn Bartholdy

■ **Gewandhaus**
Augustusplatz 8 (Mitte)
Tel. 0341/1270280
▲ Augustusplatz
www.gewandhaus.de

Long-established concert hall, where the famous Gewandhaus Orchestra, the MDR Orchestra and Thomanerchor, as well as renowned guest performers, play.

■ **Gohliser Schlösschen**
Menckestrasse 23 (Gohlis)
Tickets: Musikalienhandlung M. Oelsner
Tel. 0341/9605656
▲ Menckestrasse, Fritz-Seger-Strasse
www.gohliser-schloss.de

In the surroundings of this little Rococo palace you can hear a wide range of classical and modern music.

■ **Hochschule für Musik und Theater**
Grassistrasse 8 (Mitte)
Tel. 0341/214455
▲ Wächterstrasse
www.hmt-leipzig.de

In the small (Kammermusiksaal) and large (Grosser Saal) halls enjoy opera and musicals, summer theatre, jazz sessions, orchestral concerts and chamber music, performed by students and teachers of the music school or well-known guest musicians.

■ **Musikalische Komödie im Haus Dreilinden**
Dreilindenstrasse 30-32 (Lindenau)
Tel. 0341/1261261
▲ Angerbrücke
www.oper-leipzig.de

A lavish and varied repertoire of operetta and musicals, performances every evening.

CENTRAL THEATER

■ **Oper Leipzig**
Augustusplatz 12 (Mitte)
Tel. 0341/1261261
▲ Augustusplatz
www.oper-leipzig.de

A 300-year-old tradition
of opera that is very
much alive today, with
a repertoire from Baroque
to contemporary.
The ballet ensemble is
one of the leading
troupes in Germany.

■ **WERK II – Kulturfabrik
Leipzig e. V.**
Kochstrasse 132
(Connewitz)
Tel. 0341/3080140
▲ Connewitz, Kreuz
www.werk-2.de

A "culture factory" on the
premises of a former state-
owned engineering plant
with a varied programme of
concerts.

Theatre & Cabaret

■ **Academixer**
Kupfergasse 2 (Mitte)
Tel. 0341/21787878
▲ Augustusplatz
www.academixer.de

Political cabaret has been
performed here for over 40
years. In addition enter-
tainment in Saxon dialect,
and literary, musical and
satirical drama is played
here in the cellar of what
was once the Dresdner Hof
trade fair house.

■ **Cammerspiele**
Kochstrasse 132 (im Werk
II-Kulturfabrik/Connewitz)
Tel. 0341/3067606
▲ Connewitz, Kreuz
www.cammerspiele.de

An independent theatre
that stages works and
adaptations by well-known
contemporary and classic
writers, as well as dramas
by lesser-known authors, in
an unconventional manner.

■ **Schauspiel Leipzig**
Bosestrasse 1 (Mitte West)
Tel. 0341/1268168
▲ Thomaskirchhof
www.schauspiel-leipzig.de

World and German
premieres, experimental
theatre, performances,
films and concerts in the
main theatre of Schauspiel
Leipzig, the municipal
ensemble under its director
Enrico Lübbe. This must be
the only theatre to employ
its own philosopher. "A
complete work of art",
writes the local
newspaper.

■ **Central Kabarett**
Markt 9 (Mitte)
Tel. 0341/52903052
▲ Goerdelerring
www.centralkabarett.de

Political satire with a
Saxon and ironic touch by
the Leipzig cabaret perfor-
mer Meigl Hoffmann, his
partner Karsten Wolf and
others above the trendy
pub *Barfusz*.

Lachmesse

Germany's biggest con-
centration of satirical
cabaret ensembles is in
Leipzig – their names
are Pfeffermühle,
Academixer, Centralka-
barett, SanftWut and
many more. And so
it was natural for the
Lachmesse (Laugh-
ter Fair), a leading
international festival
of cabaret and fringe
performing arts, to be
founded here. It all
began in summer 1991,
when Swiss clown
Palino built a tower of
chairs, and people from
the Leipzig theatre
scene spontaneously
initiated a festival
with a colourful mix
of diverse rib-tickling,
clowning, political
cabaret and comedy on
the programme. Today
the big names of the
cabaret scene and up-
and-coming talent take
the stage each October.
It starts with the
award of the coveted
Leipziger Löwenzahn
(dandelion), which
goes to the best act
from the previous year's
Lachmesse.

www.lachmesse.de

Culture

Political cabaret with a Saxon slant, with more to say than just the usual east-and-west laments.

Die Prinzen

"The Princes" are an a capella group that formed in 1987 after training in the Thomanerchor, the Kreuzchor in Dresden and at Leipzig music school. Their best-known hits are *Du musst ein Schwein sein* (You Must be a Swine), *Alles nur geklaut* (I Stole It All) and *Küssen verboten* (No Kissing). Sebastian Krumbiegel, Jens Sembdner and Wolfgang Lenk were first noticed for the song *I'm the Best-looking Boy in the GDR*, but the real breakthrough came in 1991 after they changed their name from Herzbuben to Die Prinzen, and Tobias Künzel joined. Today, with 14 Golden Discs and six Platinum Discs to their name, there is more rock in the music and more edge in the lyrics, but Die Prinzen remain one of the most successful German pop bands.

www.dieprinzen.de

■ Kellertheater
Augustusplatz 12 (Mitte)
Tel. 0341/1261261
▲ Augustusplatz
www.oper-leipzig.de

The opera studio theatre is a venue for, among other events, performances by the children's choir, Heike Hennig & Co, and a Forum for Contemporary Dance and Music with the OPER Leipzig unplugged programme.

■ Krystallpalast Varieté
Magazingasse 4 (Mitte)
Tel. 0341/140660
▲ Moritzbastei, Rossplatz
www.krystallpalast.de

Compère, chansonniers, acrobats and comedians ensure you have an entertaining evening in this variety theatre.

■ Leipziger Funzel
Nikolaistrasse 6-10 (Strohsackpassage/Mitte)
Tel. 0341/9603232
▲ Augustusplatz
www.leipziger-funzel.de

A pub with cabaret, where hearty meals are served and no-one can keep a straight face.

■ Leipziger Brettl
Kleine Wintergartenbühne
Tel. 0341/9613547
Odermannstrasse 12
▲ Lindenauer Markt
www.leipzigerbrettl.de

■ Lofft
Lindenauer Markt 21 (Lindenau)
Tel. 0341/35595510
▲ Lindenauer Markt
www.lofft.de

The venue for rehearsals and performances of Freie Darstellende Kunst, who present drama, dance and performance.

■ Pfeffermühle
Katharinenstraße 17 (Mitte)
Tel. 0341/9603196
▲ Gottschedstrasse
www.kabarett-leipziger-pfeffermuehle.de

The longest-established cabaret in Leipzig, an emblem of the city in the days of the GDR.

■ SanftWut
Mädler-Passage/Grimmaische Strasse 2–4 (Mitte)
Tel. 0341/9612346
▲ Augustusplatz
www.kabarett-theater-sanftwut.de

A home for cabaret and musical theatre, with guest appearances by many other artists.

■ **theater.FACT**
Hainstrasse 1 (Mitte)
Tel. 0341/9614080
▲ Goerdelerring
www.theater-fact.de

Small comedy venue with an entertaining programme in Barthels Hof.

Hochschule für Musik und Theater

■ **theaterkompanieleipzig**
Göschenstrasse 12 (Thonberg)
Tel. 0341/9602654
▲ Gerichtsweg
www.theaterkompanie.de

This ensemble puts on contemporary drama and fairy tales for its Leipzig audiences.

Literature

■ **Literaturhaus Leipzig**
Gerichtsweg 28 (Thonberg)
Tel. 0341/9954134
▲ Gutenbergplatz
www.haus-des-buches-leipzig.de

The venue for all lovers of literature.

Cinemas

■ **CineStar**
Petersstrasse 44 (Mitte)
Tel. 01805/118811
▲ Wilhelm-Leuschner-Platz
www.cinestar.de

The latest cinema releases on a big screen!

■ **Cineding**
Karl-Heine-Strasse 83 (Plagwitz)
Tel. 0341/23959474
▲ Elster-Passage
www.cineding-leipzig.de

A little arthouse cinema with two screens and a small bistro, the heart of the scene in the west of Leipzig.

■ **Kinobar Prager Frühling**
Bernhard-Göring-Strasse 152 (Connewitz)
Tel. 0341/3065333
▲ Connewitzer Kreuz
www.kinobar-leipzig.de

Small, high-class cinema with beer garden.

■ **Passage Kinos**
Hainstrasse 19a (Mitte)
Tel. 0341/2173865
▲ Goerdelerring
www.passage-kinos.de

Traditional Leipzig cinema with a modern programme!

■ **Schauburg**
Antonienstrasse 21 (Kleinzschocher)
Tel. 0341/4244641
▲ Adler
www.schauburg-leipzig.de

For those who like movies the good old-fashioned way, this Art Deco screen with Leipzig's most comfortable cinema seats is just the place.

Deutsche Nationalbibliothek

Everything that has been published in Germany since 1913 – in German and other languages, as well as foreign literature in German translation and translations of works written in German – is collected here, documented in the national bibliography and made available to the public. The institution has been called the Deutsche National-

bibliothek since 2006. It was founded in Leipzig in 1912 as the Deutsche Bücherei, supplemented in the west after the war in 1947 by the Deutsche Bibliothek based in Frankfurt am Main, and merged with the latter after German reunification. Its seat is once again Leipzig, where the main building from 1914–16 and three previous extensions has been extended for the fourth time, in order to accommodate total holdings of at present 28.7 million items.

www.d-nb.de

Museums

The exhibits in Leipzig's museums range from antiquity to modern times, from books to cameras and even original sites.

Garden allotments

The German word for an allotment, Schrebergarten, derives from the name of a Leipzig doctor, Moritz Schreber. A friend of his, a headmaster called Hauschild, founded a school society, which he named Schreberverein, in association with parents to provide children with places to play. In 1865 the first Schreber playground was inaugurated in the Johanna-Park in Leipzig. It was a field where the children of factory workers could play and do gymnastics, supervised by teachers. In order to occupy the children, the teacher Heinrich Karl Gesell later established gardens, where whole families could pass spare time. When these gardens were divided into plots and fenced in, the allotment had come into being.

■ Ägyptisches Museum der Universität Leipzig
Goethestrasse 2 (Mitte)
▲ Augustusplatz
◆ Tue–Fri 1pm–5pm, Sat–Sun 10am–1pm
www.gko.uni-leipzig.de/ aegyptisches-museum

A collection displaying Egyptian culture from five millennia, from the pre-dynastic period up to the late kingdoms.

■ Asisi Panometer
Richard-Lehmann-Strasse 114 (Südvorstadt)
▲ Richard- Lehmann-Strasse/Arthur-Hoffmann-Strasse
Tue–Fri 10am–5pm, Sat–Sun 10am–6pm
www.asisi.de

The world's largest 360° panorama image is a view of the Titanic from a 6-metre-high platform.

■ Bach-Museum
➤ p. 12 f.

■ Coffee Baum Museum
➤ p. 12

■ Deutsches Buch- und Schriftmuseum
in the Deutsche Bücherei, Deutscher Platz 1 (Thonberg)
▲ Deutsche National-bibliothek
◆ Mon-Wed, Fri-Sun 10am-6pm, Thu 10am-8pm
www.d-nb.de

Exhibition on and documentation of valuable examples of paper, publishing and manuscripts.

■ Deutsches Kleingärtner-museum
Aachener Strasse 7 (Mitte West)
▲ Sportforum
◆ Tue-Thu 10am-4pm
www.kleingarten-museum.de

Exhibition on the history of the allotment gardening movement in the home of the first allotment gardeners' association of 1864.

■ Forum 1813
➤ p. 22

■ Grassimuseum
➤ p. 26 f.

■ Deutsches Fotomuseum
Raschwitzer Strasse 11-13 (Markkleeberg)
▲ Markkleeberg
◆ Tue-Sun 1-6pm
www.fotomuseum.eu

This collection of 600 vintage cameras, accessories and historic photographs was assembled by the cameraman and photographer Peter Langner.

■ Kunsthalle der Sparkasse
Otto-Schill-Strasse 4a (Mitte-West)
▲ Thomaskirche
◆ Tue-Thu, Sun 10a-6pm, Wed 10am-8pm
www.kunsthalle-sparkasse.de

In addition to special exhibitions and events, this collection provides a survey of and insights into the generations of Leipzig School artists.

■ **Kunstkraftwerk Leipzig**
Saalfelder Strasse 8b
(Lindenau)
tel. 0341 – 52950895
▲ S-Bahnhof Plagwitz,
Lindenau Bushof
*www.kunstkraftwerk-leipzig.
com*

A new hub of the scene for
contemporary art and cultural
events in what used to be a
gas-fired power station.

■ **Museum der Bildenden
Künste**
➤ p. 36 f.

■ **Museum für Druckkunst**
➤ p. 33

■ **Museum in der
„Runden Ecke"**
Dittrichring 24 (Mitte)
▲ Goerdelerring
◆ 10-18 Uhr, free admission
www.runde-ecke-leipzig.de

Place of memorial in what
were the rooms of the
Leipzig branch of the Stasi
(GDR Ministry for State
Security), with information
about the methods and
history of the Stasi.

■ **Naturkundemuseum
Leipzig**
Lortzingstrasse 3 (Mitte)
◆ Tue–Thu 9am–6pm
(summer), 9am–4.30pm
(winter), Fri 9am–1pm, Sat-
Sun 10am–4.30pm
naturkundemuseum.leipzig.de

A municipal regional
museum with geological,
botanical, zoological and
archaeological collec-

tions. It is famous for the
taxidermical exhibits of the
University of Leipzig.

■ **Reichsgerichtsmuseum**
➤ p. 23

■ **Sächsisches Apotheken-
museum**
Thomaskirchhof 12 (Mitte)
▲ Leuschnerplatz
◆ Tue–Wed, Fri–Sun 11am–
5pm, Thu 2pm–8pm
www.apothekenmuseum.de

Everything about the his-
tory of Saxon pharmacies
in the historic building of
the Central-Apotheke.

■ **Schillerhaus**
Menckestrasse 42
▲ Menckestrasse, Fritz-
Seger-Strasse
◆ Tue–Sun 10am–5pm
(April–Oct), Wed–Sun
11am–4pm (Nov–March)
*www.stadtgeschichtliches-
museum-leipzig.de/
schillerhaus*

An exhibition at the
original place where
Friedrich Schiller stayed
in 1785. It presents the
poet's work during his
time in Gohlis.

■ **Stadtgeschichtliches
Museum**
➤ p. 11

■ **Zeitgeschichtliches
Forum**
➤ p. 14

Botanischer Garten
The botanical garden
of the University of
Leipzig is an excellent
place to visit if you
would like to undertake
a journey around the
different vegetation
zones of the earth
and marvel at the
diversity of their plant
life. Founded over 400
years ago as a *hortus
medicus* near St Paul's
Monastery, and planted
with medicinal and
culinary herbs, it is
one of Europe's oldest
university gardens.
Since 1877 it has oc-
cupied a three-hectare
site between Johannis-
allee and Linnéstrasse,
where more than 7000
species of plant from
all over the world
thrive – from
huge old
trees to
car-
nivorous
plants
and
micro-
orchids.
Its high-
lights
include
the butterfly
house, apoth-
ecary's garden and the
garden of scent and
touch.

Linnéstrasse 1
▲ Ostplatz, Johannis-
allee,
◆ 9am-4.30pm
(Winter)
9am-6pm (Summer)
*www.uni-leipzig.de/
bota*

shopping

A variety of shops in the city centre and suburbs have unusual ideas for souvenirs to take home from Leipzig.

Porsche
The Porsche factory in Leipzig, production site for the Cayenne, Panamera, Macan and until 2006 for the limited-edition high-performance sports car Carrera GT, is more than just an assembly line – it is an invitation to experience the world of Porsche. Tours of the factory offer you an exclusive glimpse behind the scenes: you can find out how the Cayenne and Panamera are made, get to know the history of the Porsche company and from the customer centre watch the activities on the running-in and test circuit. Does that sound good? If so, you can of course try out for yourself the special handling characteristics of any Porsche model as driver or co-driver.

www.porsche-leipzig. com

■ **A Priori**
Gottschedstrasse 12
(Mitte-Süd)
▲ Gottschedstrasse
◆ Mon–Fri 10am–7pm,
Sat 10am–4pm

An El Dorado for cooks, full of high-class products for the kitchen.

■ **Comic Combo**
Riemannstraße 31
(Mitte-Süd)
▲ Hohe Strasse LVB
◆ Mon–Fri 11.30am–7pm,
Sat 10am–3pm

Fans of comics will find an unlimited selection here.

■ **Culinaris Küchenaccessoires**
Grimmaische Strasse 25
(Mitte)
▲ Markt
◆ Mon–Sat 10am–8pm

Knives, pepper mills or dishes for children – here you can find all sorts of kitchen items.

■ **Der Englandladen**
Gottschedstrasse 12
(Mitte-Süd)
▲ Gottschedstrasse
◆ Mon–Fri 10.30am–7pm,

Instead of taking home Saxon specialities, come here to buy typically English treats such as biscuits, marmalade, tea and other souvenirs.

■ **FlamingoCat**
Kurt Eisner Strasse 17
(Südvorstadt)
▲ Karl-Liebknecht-/Kurt-Eisner-Strasse
◆ Mon–Fri 11am–7pm

Hand-crafted acrylic and wooden jewellery, made and sold in an old butcher's shop.

■ **Goethe Schokoladen-taler-Manufaktur**
Markt 11-13
(Marktgalerie/Mitte)
▲ Markt
◆ Mon–Sat 10am–8pm

A little-known tip for connoisseurs of exquisite chocolate: pralines, truffles, bars of chocolate, chocolate sandwich spread and other cocoa-based magic, all produced on site by hand.

Gourmetage
Mädler Passage/Grimmais-che Strasse 2-4 (Mitte)
▲ Markt
◆ Mon–Sat 9.30am–8pm

An exclusive shop filled with all sorts of treats and specialities, from champagne to whisky, from cigars to oil, pasta and chocolate.

Hafen
Merseburger Straße 38 (Plagwitz)
▲ Karl-Heine-Straße 7 Merseburger Straße
◆ Tue-Fri 1-7pm, Sat 11am-5pm

For silk-screen prints, jewellery, stationery or clothing, in this shop you will find unusual gifts, everything made by hand, from one-off items to extremely small series.

Meissener Porzellan – Bodo Zeidler GmbH
Markt 1 (Mitte)
▲ Markt
◆ Mon–Fri 10am–7pm, Sat 10am–4pm

Whether you prefer a medallion with a portrait of Bach or a plate with his signature, or some other product of the Meissen porcelain manufactory, this is the place to buy it.

Spielerei
Karl-Liebknecht-Strasse 30 (Mitte-Süd)
▲ Hohe Strasse/LVB
◆ Mon–Fri 10am–6pm, Sat 10am–13

Toys and everything a child's heart desires.

Stretchcat
Karl-Liebknecht-Strasse 102 (Südvorstadt)
▲ Südplatz
◆ Tue-Sat 1-7pm

Retro shop on the KarLi: shelves, lamps, audio equipment and more to recreate the mood of past decades.

Zeidler Holzkunst
Im Alten Rathaus 1
▲ Markt
◆ Mon–Fri 10am–6.30pm, Sat 10am–4pm

From rabbits with pointed ears to angels and music boxes, all the traditional products of folk art from the Erzgebirge region are on sale here.

BMW
Up to 860 cars of the BMW 1 and 2 Series are manufactured in the classic production every day. In addition, two trendsetting vehicles with alternative drive systems and innovative light weight carbon bodies are produced. At the centre of the site between the big production halls lies

the office and communications building designed by the London architect Zaha Hadid. It links the three core production facilities – bodywork, paintshop and assembly – and acts as the communications hub for the whole plant. The bodywork is transported here openly and visibly, so that the production activities are transparent and can be experienced by employees and visitors at all times. Special tours of the factory provide insights into automobile production.

www.bmw-werk-leipzig.de

Addresses

German Football Association

As football was played in more and more cities of the German Reich in the late 19th century and many football clubs were founded, the idea was conceived of forming an association to represent them all. On 28 January 1900, 36 delegates from 86 clubs in Germany and abroad met under the chairmanship of E. J. Kirmse, president of the Leipzig Football Association, at the *Mariengarten* inn in Leipzig and founded

the German Football Association (Deutscher Fussball-Bund, DFB). Ferdinand Hueppe from DFV Prag was elected its first president. Just three years later the first German championship was held, with VfB Leipzig emerging victorious. Today a bronze plaque at Büttnerstrasse no. 10 serves as a reminder of the place where the DFB was founded. It now represents 26,000 clubs with 6.3 million members.

www.dfb.de

■ Information
Leipzig Tourismus und Marketing GmbH
Augustusplatz 9
04109 Leipzig
Tel. 0341/7104-260
Fax 0341/7104271
www.ltm-leipzig.de
Tourist-Information
Katharinenstraße 8
◆ Mon-Fri 9.30am-6pm,
Sat 9.30am–4pm,
Sun 9.30am–3pm

■ Banks
◆ The banks in Leipzig have the customary opening hours (usually 9am–4pm).

■ Deutsche Bahn
Tel. 0180/5996633
www.bahn.de

■ Airport
Tel. 0341/2240
www.leipzig-halle-airport.de

■ Leipzig Card
Tourists and citizens of Leipzig who want to discover their own city can buy the Leipzig Card for either one or three days. It provides free journeys on all tram lines and bus lines within the Leipzig city limits, discounts on bus tours and guided walks, reduced admission to festivals, concerts, theatres and cabarets, as well as lower prices when buying souvenirs at the tourist information office, selected retail outlets and for eating at certain restaurants. The Leipzig Card is available from the tourist information office, in the LVB (transport authority) mobility centre at main railway station, at LVB service centre at Wilhelm-Leuschner-Platz, in some hotels and via internet.
www.leipzig.travel/ leipzigcard

■ Ticket sales
CULTON Ticket
Petersssteinweg 9
Tel. 0341/141618
www.culton.de
MAWI Concert GmbH
Arndtstrasse 10,
Tel. 0341/484000
www.mawi-concert.de
Musikalienhandlung M. Oelsner
Schillerstrasse 5
Tel. 0341/9605656
www.m-oelsner.de
Ticketgalerie
Hainstrasse 1 (Barthels Hof), Tel. 0341/141414
www.ticketgalerie.de
Ticket-Service
Katharinenstraße 8
Tel. 0341/7104-260 or 265
www.leipzig.travel

■ Media
Newspapers:
Leipziger Rundschau,
Leipziger Volkszeitung,
Leipziger Wochenkurier
Radio: Mitteldeutscher
Rundfunk, Radio PSR,
Energy Sachsen, Radio
Leipzig, Mephisto 97,6

■ Hire cars
Avis: Tel. 01806/217702
Europcar:
Tel. 040/520188000
Hertz: Tel. 01806/333535
Sixt: Tel. 01806/252525

■ Emergency
Police: Tel. 110
Fire: Tel. 112
Emergency doctor:
Tel. 116117
Emergency dentist:
Tel. 0341/3190290
Emergency pharmacy:
www.aponet.de
ADAC breakdown service:
Tel. 01802/222222
Lost and found:
Tel. 0341/1238400

■ Public transport
Leipziger Verkehrsbetriebe
Karl-Liebknecht-Strasse 12
04107 Leipzig
Service phone: 0341/19449
www.lvb.de

LVB Mobility Centre at the
railway station
◆ Mon–Fri 8am–8pm,
Sat 8am–4pm

LVB service centre
Petersstrasse/Markgrafen-
strasse
◆ Mon–Fri 8am–8pm,
Sat 8am–4pm

■ City tours
Leipzig Details
Tel. 0341/3039112
www.leipzigdetails.de
Leipzig erleben
Tel. 0341/7104230
www.leipzig-erleben.com
lipzi tours
Guided tour by bike
Tel. 0341/2239482
www.lipzitours.de
Stadttouren
Monika Auspurg
Tel. 0341/9411775
www.stadttouren-leipzig.de
Treffpunkt Leipzig
Tel. 0341/1497879
www.treffpunktleipzig.de

■ Taxi
**Leipzig's oldest taxi
service centre**
Tel. 0341/4884
Mini Car Leipzig
Tel. 0341/2511211
Taxi direct
Tel. 0341/ 86329777 oder
0175/2321458
Taxi mit der Mütze
Tel. 0341/ 4233
**Taxi & car hire service
Dietmar Feustel**
Tel. 0341/8696999

■ Websites
In English
www.leipzig.de/int/en/
www.leipziger-messe.de
www.leipziginfo.de
www.uni-leipzig.de
In German
www.leipzig-lexikon.de
www.leipzig-online.de
www.leipzig-sachsen.de
www.l-iz.de

The Saxon dialect ...
... is not just the way
people speak in and
around Leipzig, but
also an essential foun-
dation of the High Ger-
man language. Because

Saxony was a prosper-
ous region in the Mid-
dle Ages where people
from all parts of the
German-speaking world
lived, a lingua franca
known as Meissen
Chancellery German
was developed that
was soon understood in
all almost parts of the
Holy Roman Empire.
This is the reason why,
for example, Luther
translated the Bible
into Saxon, which
helped to establish the
dialect increasingly as
the standard version of
German.

Leipzig's History

6th century   Slavs settle near the confluence of the Elster and Parthe and call their village Lipzi (an old Sorbian word for lime tree).

1015   First mention of the castle Urbs Libzi in the chronicle of Bishop Thietmar of Merseburg.

1165   Margrave Otto the Rich of Meissen grants a town charter to Urbs Libzi and gives it permission to hold a market.

1268   An edict on the right of escorted passage lays the basis for the start of long-distance trade.

1273   Leipzig gains the right to mint coins.

1409   Foundation of the University of Leipzig.

1458   Leipzig's New Year market is the third permitted trade fair.

1481   First book printed in Leipzig.

1485   Saxony is divided between the Albertine and Ernestine lines; Leipzig belongs to the former.

1497   Emperor Maximilian I grants an imperial trade fair privilege.

1519   Disputation between Martin Luther and Johannes Eck at the Pleissenburg.

1539   The Reformation comes to Leipzig.

1595   Foundation of the Leipzig guild of book printers.

1660   Leipziger Zeitung, the world's first daily newspaper.

1693   First opera house opens on Brühl.

1723   Bach becomes cantor of St Thomas' Church and director of city music.

1743   The Grosses Concert is the forerunner of the Gewandhaus Orchestra.

1813   At the Battle of the Nations the allied armies of Russia, Prussia, Austria and Sweden oppose Napoleon's forces.

1825	Association of German booksellers founded in Leipzig.
1842	Bayerischer Bahnhof, Germany's oldest surviving railway terminus, goes into operation.
1895	The sample fair replaces the old goods fair.
1920	Construction of Leipzig's Technische Messe begins.
1938	Under Nazi rule Leipzig becomes the Reich trade fair city.
1945	The US Army occupies Leipzig. According to the decisions of the Yalta Conference, Leipzig is part of the Soviet-occupied zone.
1952	Leipzig becomes capital of a region of the GDR.
1954	Exhibitors from 37 and visitors from 59 countries take part in the Leipzig autumn fair.
1959	A book fair takes place once again.
1968	St Paul's Church is demolished at the behest of the SED party leadership.
1989	Citizens of Leipzig demonstrate for reforms in the GDR and play a decisive role in the fall of the Wall with their Monday prayers.
1996	Opening of the new trade fair grounds.
2002	Porsche comes to Leipzig.
2005	The new BMW plant opens.
2006	five matches in the football World Cup were played in the new Zentralstadion.
2008	the Leipzig logistics hub of DHL was opened.
2012	The Augusteum and the Paulinum of the university are finished.
2013	The City Tunnel is opened.
2015	Leipzig celebrates its 1000th anniversary.

Index

Picture Credits